Praise for K-State's Wrestling Legacy...

"I competed against Kansas State during college. Sadly, the program was dropped, but wrestling fans in Kansas and nationwide will get a lot out of Pat Kelly's book. It is an entertaining and interesting read full of historical information not only about Kansas State and the sport of wrestling but also events and personalities that will motivate readers in their personal and professional lives."

–Dan Gable

1968 and 1969 NCAA Champion for Iowa State, 1972 Olympic Champion,
coached the Iowa Hawkeyes to 15 NCAA titles,
distinguished member of the National Wrestling Hall of Fame,
Presidential Medal of Freedom recipient

"Patrick Kelly's penchant for wanting to know more is extremely evident in this book. As a wrestling historian, I understand the reaction to feeling like you don't know the answer. Now, when people ask about the history of Kansas State wrestling, people around the state and the country have a resource to not only learn, but to be able to re-tell the stories contained within. Wrestling is full of colorful and unique personalities and Patrick's delivered the stories and personalities with K-State wrestling's short, but interesting history to the community. It's one of those books you will read once but refer to it constantly in the future."

–Jason Bryant

Wrestling historian, award-winning journalist,
public address announcer for numerous NCAA championships
and the London, Rio, and Paris Olympics

"It might be considered a minor sport to some, but it is not a minor sport to wrestlers and dedicated wrestling fans, including the Keller family of St. Francis, Kansas. The two of us brothers became wrestlers and wrestling fans before we started kindergarten because of the influence of our Dad, Ed Keller. He was a member of the first wrestling team at St. Francis High School and was the captain of K-State's Big 6 championship wrestling team in 1939. After being a part of state championship teams at St. Francis, we followed in Dad's footsteps and wrestled at K-State. The work that Pat Kelly has done to research the history of K-State wrestling and describe its part in the development of wrestling in Kansas is a true labor of love. The details he has documented, the great stories, and the broad influence of K-State wrestling should not be forgotten. Any fan of wrestling in Kansas should read Pat's book and make sure the history is preserved. Who knows, K-State may be able to bring back wrestling someday and add to the history so well-documented in this book."

−Tom Keller and Bill Keller
KSU wrestling 1966-1970 and 1968-1972, respectively

"…a fascinating journey about a forgotten wrestling program. Who knew that some of the most influential wrestlers attended Kansas State?"

−Kyle Klingman
Wrestling journalist, former Director of the
National Wrestling Hall of Fame Dan Gable Museum,
co-author of A Wrestling Life 2 *and* Do It Anyway

"Buel Patterson was an important part of Illinois wrestling history. It was interesting to learn of his impact on Kansas wrestling during the early part of his career. A well-researched book and captivating for any wrestling enthusiast."

−Joe Cliffe
High school coach in Illinois for over 40 years,
Illinois Wrestling Coaches and Officials Association Hall of Fame,
National High School Athletic Coaches Association Hall of Fame

"Kansas State wrestling, unfortunately, is no longer with us, but Patrick Kelly tells its story well. Interesting to many Oklahoma and Oklahoma State wrestling fans is their unique intertwinement. From coaching connections, athletes, a shared conference, geography, and more. The programs have had a substantial impact on each other that even I didn't know before reading this book."

—Seth Duckworth
OWrestle.com, *2022 National Wrestling Media Association Journalist of the Year*

K-State's Wrestling Legacy

Stories, Stats, and Personalities that Shaped the Sport in Kansas and Beyond

Patrick Kelly

Flint Hills Publishing

K-State's Wrestling Legacy
Stories, Stats, and Personalities that Shaped the Sport in Kansas and Beyond
© 2025 by Patrick Kelly

Cover Design by Amy Albright

ῑFlint Hills Publishing

Topeka, Kansas
Tucson, Arizona
www.flinthillspublishing.com

Printed in the U.S.A.

Paperback Book: ISBN: 978-1-966323-05-1

LCCN 2024926929

DEDICATION

To Lisa, Ryan, Bailey, and Ella.
Thanks for always being in my corner.

To Marlys and Paul Kelly.
Your encouragement and support continue to
bolster me long after your earthly days.

To Karen, Con, Tim, Jeff, Mike, Steve, Kristie, and Mark.
By the accident of birth, I won the sibling lottery.

To Coach Al DeLeon.
If I believed in myself half as much as you believed in me,
I would have moved mountains. Rest in Peace.

To Coach Mike Denney.
It was an honor and a privilege to enter your world.
Everyone should be so lucky. "OOOSSS!"

CONTENTS

FOREWARD

From National Wrestling Hall of Famer,
Mike Chapman

By his own words, family, faith, and wrestling have defined Pat Kelly's entire life. And for those who know him, he has been an excellent role model in all three areas.

He was born and raised in Britt, Iowa, which has been a hotbed of wrestling for decades. The small town of just two thousand citizens has produced many wrestling champions, including Bob Steenlage, Iowa's first four-time state champion who went on to become an All-American at West Point.

Pat's dad wrestled in high school and for two years at Iowa State and developed a love for the sport that he passed on to his family. Pat first stepped onto a mat at age five and eventually won two state titles for Britt High School, under the tutelage of Al DeLeon, who had been a two-time All-American for Mankato State in the early 1960s.

Pat was a member of the Iowa Hawkeyes with Coach Dan Gable for three and a half years then transferred to the University of Nebraska at Omaha, where he became a two-time All-American at the NCAA Division II level for Coach Mike Denney.

He entered the education field and has taught and coached at various levels in Kansas, Iowa, and Nebraska for thirty years, including seventeen combined years as head coach in Kansas at Newton High School and Seaman High School, the latter for fourteen years.

With that tremendous background to draw upon, he branched out into other areas to help promote the sport he loves. He has written many articles for *WIN* (*Wrestling Insider Newsmagazine*) and has produced over two hundred podcast episodes for the Kansas Wrestling Coaches Association (KWCA) and USA Wrestling-Kansas (USAWKS).

He has always considered himself a student of the sport and has collected numerous magazine articles and wresting books for decades. He says that when his peers were saving baseball cards and studying Super Bowl lineups, he knew who the NCAA champs and Olympic wrestlers were. And at age sixteen, he set a goal of writing a book about some phase of the sport of wrestling.

This book is the result of that commitment, forged from many years of study and research. As an author myself, I know the energy and determination that goes into such a work.

Pat and Lisa, his wife of thirty years, have three grown children and Pat says that any successes they all have experienced are the direct result of a strong Catholic faith that has held the family together.

I learned some fascinating stories about wrestling in the book and I am proud to have played a very minor role in this massive project by Pat Kelly. I highly recommend it to all fans of the sport, from any part of the country!

—Mike Chapman
creator of *W.I.N Magazine*, the Dan Hodge Trophy,
the Dan Gable Museum, and author of 32 books

PROLOGUE
From the Author

Since first moving to Kansas in 1998, I had been casually interested in the story of the Kansas State University wrestling program. It wasn't until I retired from coaching at the high school level in 2022 that I dove deeper into the topic. I was hooked from the start. The personalities, the connections, and the unique stories kept me motivated and intrigued.

I realized early on that this was a story with depth and breadth even beyond Kansas State University that needed to be told sooner rather than later. 2025 marks fifty years since the program was dropped. Fifty! Waiting too much longer meant that there would be fewer first-hand accounts that bring the stats and newspaper articles to life. The project consumed time formerly spent on my coaching duties. The pursuit had similarities between competing and coaching. There were wins, setbacks, late nights, surprise discoveries, and a desire to get the job done.

My motives were simple: preserve the program's history and honor those who participated in it. Kansas State University Wrestling began in 1922 and ended in 1975. I tasked myself with providing the reader with an accurate, interesting, and entertaining historical perspective. I hope that this book has checked those boxes.

My motives were not and are not rooted in reinstating the program. That would have taken away from my stated objectives of preserving and honoring. My energies were focused on the "what was."

Of the four men's sports that were dropped at K-State during the 1974-75 school year, only golf has been reinstated. Wrestling, gymnastics, and tennis have all been dormant since then. On the women's side, gymnastics, softball, and swimming were offered in 1975 but are no longer part of the landscape. However, soccer (added in 2016), rowing (added in 1996), and golf (added in 1981), are now part of women's athletics at K-State.

Maintaining athletic programs in the current environment on

major college campuses is a fundraising strain. Keeping up with the competition while remaining competitive in the era of Name, Image, and Likeness (NIL), the NCAA transfer portal, and runaway salaries for basketball and football coaches has created its own industry. Adding programs is a multi-layered, complex process that armchair Athletic Directors (ADs) can't begin to understand.

If wrestling returns to K-State at some point, that would be great. If not, let's continue to honor the past and take pride in what once was. As frustrating as it may be that wrestling doesn't exist at K-State or any other NCAA DI institution in the state, recognizing and honoring the past is important on its own and as a reference for the build-back cause.

A special thanks goes to the staff at the K-State Library and archives. It takes a village, and they were literally like having a staff. Thanks to the Kansas Historical Society State Archives for showing me the way to resources that brought decades-old stories to life. Thank you, Collegian Media Group, for permission to use images in the K-State collection to help bring the stories to life. To Benjamin Hedges, Oklahoma State University and the OSU Archives for providing information and permission to use images that helped demonstrate the OSU/K-State connection. Mike Chapman's insight, encouragement, and stamp of approval were the push that turned this "hobby project" into the professional piece it became. Mitch Beims constructed and maintains the Kansas High School Wrestling State Placers website, found at www.kansashswrestling.com. Every state should have such an organized and comprehensive database of historic records. Hats off, Mitch! Thanks for the support of USA-Wrestling Kansas. To Catherine Baker Nicholson, thank you for your help with the writing process and input on your grandfather, Bill Doyle's chapter. I encourage everyone to pick up her book *Running in Borrowed Shoes: Thane Baker and the 1952 Summer Games*. It is a captivating look at her father, who happens to be K-State's most decorated track and field athlete. Also, thanks to Richard Frakes for his help on the accuracy of Bill Doyle's career accomplishments at Douglass High School. Most of all, thank you to the alumni and associates of the program for their willingness to participate and for their support. It was an honor and a privilege to meet you. Tom and Bill Keller, Dee Gard, Wayne Jackson, Richard DeMoss, Pat Doyle, Fred Fozzard, and Jamie Garten were positive forces to kickstart the process. I'm forever grateful for their support and enthusiasm for the project.

Finally, Coach Buel "Pat" Patterson deserves his own chapter (maybe his own book). His early influence on the sport of wrestling at K-State and the state of Kansas is so prevalent that it is part of the sport's very identity in the Sunflower State. However, to leave him out of other chapters to preserve his information for his own would be turning those chapters into Swiss cheese. The Mt. Rushmore of Kansas Wrestling certainly has Pat as its George Washington.

Enjoy!

-1-
A Brief History

The exact origin of the Kansas State University wrestling program is unclear. A passage from the 1925 *Royal Purple* student yearbook stated: "This is the third year that inter-collegiate wrestling has been in existence at KSAC." KSAC, for reference, is the abbreviated form of Kansas State Agriculture College, which preceded the current Kansas State University and Kansas State College of Agriculture and Applied Sciences, used from 1931-1959.[1] That article would date the program's start to the 1922-23 school year. However, a passage in the 1927 *Royal Purple* notes: "Inter-Collegiate wrestling was taken up on an extensive scale for the first time during 1926-27."

Since roster references were made and the first competition held during the 1922-23 school year (a 31-0 dual loss to Kansas University on Monday, March 5, 1923), that is what will be recognized as the first wrestling team in Kansas State University history in this publication. With that said, the team did not participate in any competitions during the 1923-24 season. A roster was listed, practices were held, and the schedule was being finalized, but injury and sickness prevented competitions from happening. Humble beginnings for certain.

Penn State marks 1908-09 as its inaugural wrestling season. The University of Iowa, 1910-11; Oklahoma State University, 1914-15; and the University of Michigan, 1922-23.

Columbia University is the self-proclaimed oldest continuous college wrestling program in the country. The Light Blue lists their first season as 1903-04. Yale shared the "first program" distinction with Columbia but dropped the sport in 1991.

Newspaper articles of the day indicate that the sport began appearing in earnest on college and university campuses across the country during the 1920s. The sport's inclusion may be related to the popularity of professional wrestling during the late 1800s and into the early 1900s. It was not uncommon for Kansas newspapers of the period to report on major national and regional matches as well as local affairs. For example, the Frank Gotch vs. George Hackenschmidt re-match of 1911 garnered a full page 1 in an extra edition of *The Wichita Beacon* on September 1st of that year.

The popularity of professional wrestling at the turn of the century was evident in newspaper accounts of the day. For example, the 1911 Frank Gotch vs. George Hackenschmidt rematch garnered an extra edition in *The Wichita Beacon*.
Photo Credit: Wichita Eagle.

Ed "Strangler" Lewis, Joe Stecher, and Earl Caddock were common names that made their way into newspapers across the state. Dr. B.F. Roller, "the Wrestling Physician" from Seattle, was also a common mention and was hyped as a threat to Gotch's title. Roller competed in Kansas regularly. Dick Daviscourt, contender for the world's wrestling championship, occasionally helped coach the Fairmont University and University of Kansas wrestlers in the 1920s. He was from California but lived part-time in Wichita.

Sol Schlegel of Topeka, Wayne Long of Burlington, Aulius Britt of Luray, Alfred Baker of Atchison, and Andy "Dutch" Snyder of Doniphan were just a few of the local names from the early 1900s familiar to wrestling enthusiasts from the Sunflower State.

Regional and local competitions were held regularly across the state in opera houses and other municipal venues. Hutchinson, Salina, and Emporia were popular smaller market locations for these competitions.

The sport was not without its dissenting voices, however. A December 7, 1912 article in *The Hutchinson News* titled "Wrestling Tabooed" told of the city commission's unanimous vote to ban wrestling matches in the city-owned convention hall due to its violent nature and gambling activity that it attracted. The article's tone was reminiscent of the early days of Mixed Martial Arts (MMA) competitions, where contests were banned in one jurisdiction and moved to another city, sometimes on the day of the event. In 1996, Arizona congressman and presidential candidate John McCain famously referred to MMA as "human cockfighting."

A history lesson is in order for those familiar with "professional" wrestling in the modern day, which has predetermined outcomes, theatrics, and style over substance.

Mike Chapman, who was kind enough to write the foreword to this book, has a good understanding of professional wrestling at the turn of the century and how it impacted colleges supporting the sport on their campuses during that era.

According to Chapman, "A lot of it was due to a very charismatic champion named Frank Gotch. He's from Humboldt, Iowa, and he was handsome, articulate, and very well-built. And remember, we are talking about an era when football and baseball were in their infancy. There was hardly any tennis or golf to speak of. The top champions, the most idolized sports heroes in America, were the heavyweight boxing champion and the heavyweight wrestling champion. Gotch was the Tom Brady of his era. Very articulate. The media attracted itself to him. The top wrestling and boxing writer of the '30s and '40s was Nat Fleischer. He even started the legendary magazine, *The Ring*, all about boxing and wrestling. In one of his books, *From Milo to Londos*, he wrote, 'It was the popularity of Frank Gotch that started many colleges to take up the sport of wrestling.' And there is a lot of truth to that. I think it was Gotch's popularity that helped it spread. So, yes, pro wrestling had a big impact on the popularity of amateur wrestling starting to expand."

An account from the 1998 documentary, *The Unreal Story of Pro Wrestling,* put it this way: "A hundred years ago, professional wrestling was the most popular spectator sport in America. Baseball was beginning to develop, but football and basketball hadn't appeared nationally. Wrestling was considered more dignified than boxing, more scientific. Stars like Frank Gotch and George Hackenschmidt drew enormous crowds to their series of championship bouts."

That thought resonated across the landscape in Kansas as well. A March 9, 1912, *Lawrence Daily Journal* article picked up on the enthusiasm of adopting wrestling on college campuses: "Wrestling is coming to be recognized as a game for inter-collegiate competition among the universities and colleges of the country and in the future may be expected to be a leader among the minor sports."

That enthusiasm showed signs of fading when fans were looking for sporting events packaged to match their schedules and passion for entertainment and pure sporting activity. Chapman, who has also been featured in several wrestling-themed documentaries, provides his analysis in the *Unreal Story of Pro Wrestling,* as to why professional wrestling as it is known today exploded in popularity when it got away from being a legitimate sporting contest and at the same time began losing favor on many college campuses: "People came at seven o'clock in the evening to spend an hour watching a wrestling match and at 12:30 a.m. they were still there. So, think about it, you're a spectator and came to see a great athletic event, and it was great, except for it lasted five hours and thirty minutes."

In a more recent interview at his home in Newton, Iowa, Chapman expanded on that thought, "Wrestling was up against a changing society where the warrior ethic started to fade away. It was tough for amateur wrestling to be exciting enough for the average American sports fan in my estimation."

The current list of twenty-four college wrestling programs in the state of Kansas (seventeen men's and seven women's programs) would be virtually unrecognizable compared to the list from the Roaring '20s. Kansas State Teachers College of Pittsburg (now Pittsburg State University), Kansas State Teachers College (now Emporia State University), The College of Emporia (closed in 1974), the University of Kansas, Hays Teachers College (now Ft. Hays State

University), and the aforementioned Fairmount College (now Wichita State University) were all part of the Kansas wrestling landscape in the 1920s, along with Kansas State. Of that list, only Ft. Hays State University still has a program; its opening season dates back to the 1926-27 school year.

As mentioned, the exact origin of the K-State wrestling program may be unclear, but without a creative and innovative professor and supportive athletic director, the program may not have gotten off the ground. Having the powerful Oklahoma A&M program just four hours down the road also proved to be a boost.

E.A. Knoth earned his undergraduate degree at the Normal College of Physical Education in Indianapolis,[2] a highly regarded program at the time. He came to Manhattan after a stint at the University of Illinois, where he coached wrestling, among other duties. He was interested in starting a wrestling program at K-State and expanding his mission of infusing physical education into the required course of study for undergrads.

Shortly after his arrival on campus, he devised a plan to make physical fitness classes and intramural athletic competitions a required part of degree completion. His efforts helped develop so-called "minor sports," of which wrestling was categorized.

Knoth, K-State's head basketball coach during the 1920-21 season, introduced intramural athletics to K-State in 1920. He included basketball, baseball, soccer, boxing, wrestling, swimming, handball, tennis, and track. A small student fee was added to the tuition cost to fund the programs. That, along with admission fees from boxing and wrestling competitions, made the program self-sustaining. By 1921, Knoth's idea of "athletics for the masses" had attracted over 1,000 students to the various sports. In December of 1922, the university announced that it was adopting Knoth's physical education class requirement for degree completion going forward from current freshmen and sophomores.

Knoth believed in what he was doing and even published a book titled *Methods of Physical Education* in 1923. The book contained chapters that included daily lesson plans, ideas for group activities, and basic instruction for teaching the rules and techniques of football, baseball, basketball, track and field, boxing, and wrestling. The final chapter details information on establishing and maintaining an intramural program at the college level modeled after what Knoth implemented at K-State.

E.A. Knoth helped get the K-State wrestling program off the ground. He started it from scratch and served as the program's first coach. *Photo Credit:* Collegiate Media Group.

Michael Ahearn, K-State's popular and charismatic athletic director, was himself a transplant. Born in Rotherham, England, in 1878, the family moved to Boston during his youth. He graduated from Massachusetts Agriculture College (now the University of Massachusetts) in 1904, where he was a standout athlete in football, basketball, baseball, tennis, and ice polo (ice hockey) while earning a degree, with honors, in horticulture.

Ahearn was hired as head football coach at Kansas State immediately after graduating from college and spent the rest of his life in Manhattan.

He coached football, basketball, baseball, tennis, and golf at K-State for several years before concentrating solely on his teaching duties in the horticulture department.

In 1920, he was sought out for the athletic director role, a position that he would remain in for the next twenty-six years. He was revered and respected far and wide for being fair and honest. He is credited with moving Kansas State athletics into the modern era with better facilities and by hiring highly regarded coaches. He became known as the "Father of Kansas State Athletics." The 1924 *Royal Purple* yearbook went as far as to call him the "Patron Saint of Aggie Athletics."

Before Athletic Director Mike Ahearn was affiliated with K-State, he was a stand-out athlete at Massachusetts Agricultural College (now the University of Massachusetts).
Photo Credit: Collegiate Media Group.

Ahearn worked with Knoth to get the wrestling program on solid footing by using the intramural program as a steppingstone to varsity competition. The winners in each weight class of the intramural tournament earned a spot in the varsity lineup during the early years. This incentive brought out large numbers to the intramural program.

Ahearn was not well-versed in wrestling but served as the Kansas representative on the National Boxing and Wrestling Association board and was savvy enough to seek out the power programs to make coaching hires. He was interested in elevating the wrestling program by hiring a coach with wrestling experience from a program that K-State could model itself after.

Knoth was also on board with the idea. He wanted to participate in the development of the program he had helped establish by hiring a coach who was singularly focused on wrestling and had a competitive background to impart the necessary knowledge and skills to the athletes. It was a rocky road, but eventually, the Cats found their guy.

Ahearn first looked to Iowa State's power program and brought Cyclone star Joe Greer to campus for the 1923-24 season. The Greer era, however, was a bust, lasting only one unsuccessful season. The program, in fact, appeared to take a step in the wrong direction under Coach Greer, who was also in the school's veterinarian program.

Knoth was interested in handing off the program but was also vested in ensuring it was in good hands. After Greer's departure, Knoth again took back the reins and remained in the head position until the completion of the 1924-25 season.

By the start of the 1925-26 season, a suitable replacement had not been found, and Knoth remained in the head coach role. However, after five and a half years at K-State, Knoth left at the end of the first semester for pursuits in private business. He began a long career with the A.G. Spalding Sporting Goods Company. He initially had a sales area spanning Arkansas and Tennessee and was also tasked with organizing baseball competitions.

Enter Frank Root and Oliver "Shorty" Walgren.

Root was a stand-out right end and halfback for the Wildcats from 1911-14. After graduating, he spent three seasons as head basketball coach at Winfield High School.

He returned to K-State in 1922, when he was added to the football coaching staff as an assistant backfield coach. Root eventually became head basketball coach from 1933-39, but in 1926, he stepped up to fill the void made by Knoth's departure.

Root joined Knoth and later Fritz Knorr as head basketball coaches who also served as head wrestling coach for the Wildcats. In Root's case, he was a "sort of" head coach. Chaperone or supervisor may be a more appropriate title. He provided quotes for newspaper articles and accompanied the team to competitions, but team captain O.E. "Shorty" Walgren was more of the coach regarding teaching technique and preparing the team for competition.

Walgren was also captain of the boxing team. He earned his DVM Degree and went on to a career as a veterinarian in Nebraska.

It was time to get serious about the wrestling program and hire a coach with the stability and wrestling knowledge to elevate the program to legitimacy. Ahearn's next move was to tap into Ed Gallagher's dynasty at Oklahoma A&M (now Oklahoma State University).

Like many athletic directors in modern times, Ahearn looked to the most successful programs in the country to draw coaching candidates. He sought out Greer from the powerful Iowa State program and then turned to *the* power program for his next two head wrestling coaches.

At the time, Ed Gallager oversaw a dynasty in college wrestling that he had created at Oklahoma A&M, and Ahearn was eager to capitalize on that success. Gallagher was born in Perth, Kansas, in 1887, an unincorporated community in Sumner County about nine miles southwest of Wellington and twenty miles north of the Oklahoma border. He graduated high school in 1905 and enrolled in the College of Engineering at Oklahoma A&M that fall.

Ed Gallager. Photo Credit: Oklahoma State University Archives

In 1909, he graduated from A&M with an electrical engineering degree. Gallagher excelled as a track athlete and on the gridiron. He was the team captain of both sports and class president. Additionally, he kept busy working his way through college to pay the bills.

Upon graduation, he began coaching track at A&M. After four years, he headed north to Baldwin City, Kansas, where he was director of athletics at Baker University for two years. He then returned to Stillwater, where he became director of physical education from 1915 to 1920. In 1920, he was elevated to Director of Athletics and Physical Education.

In 1916, Gallagher was also put in charge of the upstart wrestling program. The following passage from *The El Reno Daily*, July 27, 1932, vividly depicts Gallagher as a coach and person.

> Gallagher became interested in wrestling for two reasons. First, in his engineering course he has studied leverage and how to make a certain force do the utmost amount of work when properly applied. He imparted these principles to members of his squad with the result that he taught them many holds and counters that won matches and championships for A&M in the second place, he learned from his studies of anatomy and human body that pressure applied to certain muscles caused them to become fatigued and by combining the results of the two observed he developed a scientific system of coaching which has never been excelled in college wrestling. Ed was never a famous wrestler and was never a contestant in an intercollegiate bout.
>
> Ed Gallagher is a well-built man of medium height and weight. He is clean of limb and moves with the ease of a schoolboy. He is keener mentally and more active physically than many men half his age and he personally directs all his physical education classes and his wrestling squad. He is a genius at organization and is perfectly cool under the most trying circumstances. His recreation is golf and he shoots in the 70s.
>
> A&M wrestling teams are handled with kindness yet firmness. Gallagher puts his men through the most grueling training and insists on the observance of the strictest rules. Yet his boys love him, and he actually treats them as a father should treat his sons. They take

their problems to him and are always certain to get the best advice. Having six children of his own, he understands the problems confronting the youth of the present day and is always ready to lend a hand on behalf of young people. As long as he is at the helm, wrestling will prosper at Oklahoma A&M. College and sport of the highest character will be the result.

He was a coach ahead of his time. Although he was never a wrestler himself, he developed the Aggies into a national power. Even today, he ranks among the elite coaches regardless of sport in collegiate athletics.

Ed Gallagher served as head coach at Oklahoma A&M from 1916 to 1940. The first NCAA wrestling championships were held in 1928. Gallagher led A&M to eleven titles and two runner-up finishes in the first thirteen years of the event. Prior to that, his teams were the perennial power when the AAU governed the national collegiate wrestling championships. *Photo Credit:* Oklahoma State University Archives.

Gallagher studied wrestling and its mechanics to develop techniques based on his research and training as an engineer. He also vested time in studying nutrition and sleep as performance enhancers. In recruiting, he looked for lean, athletic body types and paid close attention to strong character and work ethic as much as high school accolades.

During the thirteen years he coached after the first NCAA-recognized national tournament in 1928, he guided the Cowboys to eleven titles and two runner-up finishes. Gallagher died in 1940 after returning from a camping venture in Colorado. The cause of death was complications from Parkinson's Disease, which forced him to give up his administrative duties in 1938. He also expected to give up coaching after the 1940-41 season.

Ahearn's first hire from Stillwater was Gerald Northrip. He was a national champion and 1925-26 Cowboy team captain. He was also a state champion for Clinton High School in Oklahoma during the first year that the school offered wrestling. He won his state championship despite not having a coach.

The 1926-27 Wildcat team finished 0-10 in duals. The program-building process may have been too much for Northrip, who, like Greer, lasted only one season in Manhattan.

In 1927, Ahearn secured the services of B.R. "Pat" Patterson to lead the wrestling team and later, the boxing program.

Before leading the K-State wrestling program for twenty years starting in 1927, Buel "Pat" Patterson was a standout on the Oklahoma A&M teams coached by Ed Gallagher. Patterson won the 1925 national championship and served as team captain during his senior season. *Photo Credit:* Oklahoma State University Archives.

Ahearn hit the jackpot with Pat. The Wildcats finally had the coach to put the team on solid footing and bring it the national recognition the fledgling program had never experienced.

Patterson was a champion wrestler for A&M and proved to be an outstanding coach, most notably bringing the campus a third-place showing at the 1931 NCAA tournament and mentoring an individual NCAA champion in Bill Doyle. He also led the program to four Big

Six titles (1929, 1931, 1939, and 1940) and four top 10 NCAA tournament finishes.

Before Patterson's arrival, the program's initial wave of interest subsided, partly due to the instability caused by a rapid succession of coaching changes.

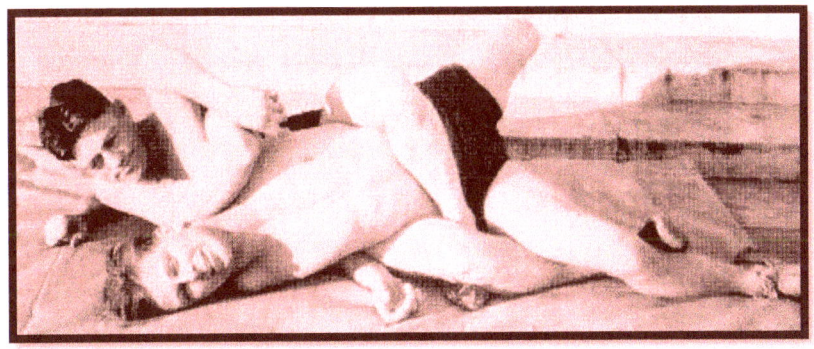

Buel "Pat" Patterson was a standout at A&M. He won the 1925 national championship at 125 pounds and was team captain during his senior season in 1927. Gallagher thought highly of his prized pupil, and many assumed Pat would be named head coach when Gallagher retired. Gallagher died in 1940, and Art Griffith was hired.
Photo Credit: Oklahoma State University Archives

A February 18, 1925, article from *The Kansas Industrialist* stated: "Intercollegiate competition in boxing and wrestling may have to be discontinued at the Kansas State Agricultural College unless more student interest is shown in these sports, according to E.A. Knoth, coach of minor sports." The article went on to elaborate:

> ...three members of the boxing team had to go on the mat to fill out the quota of K.S.A.C entrants in the wrestling tournament with the University of Kansas team Saturday night. Swimming and tennis as minor sports at the college have provoked much wider interest than boxing and wrestling.

Patterson spent twenty seasons in Manhattan before moving on to the University of Nebraska for three years and the University of Illinois for eighteen. He led the Cornhuskers to a Big Seven Championship in 1949 and the Illini to a Big 10 title in 1952. He retired from the University of Illinois in 1968.

During the 1930s and into the 1940s, wrestling was on the rise at Kansas State under Pat's direction. The 1939 Royal Purple yearbook had high praise for the direction the wrestling program was heading:

> Wrestling, a booming sport at Kansas State for several seasons, hit a climax this year when Coach B.R. Patterson's men won the Big Six championship and record-breaking crowds of 1,200 to 1,500 attended home dual meets in Nichols Gym.

An article in the July 30, 1939 edition of *The Morning Chronicle* confirmed that idea:

> Wrestling—a booming sport which drew record crowds to Nichols gymnasium last year—reached a climax when the Wildcats won the Big Six championship under the guidance of their popular coach, B.R. "Pat" Paterson. Wrestling is approaching basketball as a popular winter sport, and Coach Patterson's well-trained men always are capable of treating the spectators to a thrilling and sportsmanlike show.

Patterson was a national figure in the sport during his coaching years as a leader, tireless promoter, and innovator. For ten years, he edited the *Official NCAA Wrestling Guide*. He served as president of the National Wrestling Coaches Association in 1939. He was involved with the NCAA Wrestling Rules Committee and served as its chairman from 1926-52. He was involved in the administration of the 1948 Olympic Wrestling team and served as chairman and manager of the 1952 Olympic Wrestling Committee, traveling to Helsinki, Finland with the team.

He is believed to be the first to use video extensively in the sport. It is documented that he was responsible for videotaping the NCAA Championships for the first time in 1937. He edited the film, cutting and titling it for distribution. As early as 1934, he hired a videographer and photographer to capture footage of the high school state wrestling tournament, which he brought into existence and managed for several years in Kansas and later Illinois.

Patterson was forward-thinking and creative. He worked to develop the Missouri Valley AAU tournament that served as a preliminary Olympic Trials qualifier in 1936. He created a tournament concept that featured unique "folkstyle" wrestling from other countries. However, it isn't clear if the tournament was brought to fruition. In 1938, he hosted an exhibition dual against Waseda University of Japan to expose his K-State athletes to international wrestling.

Patterson worked to elevate wrestling and boxing competitions to entertainment options for spectators rather than drawn-out, no-frills events. He even made challenge matches and boxing matches well-attended campus activities for students.

His efforts to offer wrestling at the high school level in Kansas brought the state its first official state tournament in 1930. His support for and promotion of starting programs at the grass-roots level in Kansas helped bring the sport along. He had a similar impact on the sport while at the University of Illinois, when he also made himself available to present at clinics and rules interpretation meetings. In Illinois, he was also manager of the high school state tournament for several years.

Patterson co-authored a book with Ray Carson, *Principles of Championship Wrestling*. Published in 1972, it presents technical instruction and psychological and training methods.

Ed Gallagher and his Oklahoma A&M Aggies had status during the pre- and early- NCAA championship era with unmatched success. Even with that reputation, Patterson stood out in Coach Gallagher's eyes. One press release quotes Gallagher as relaying that Patterson was "one of the most clever wrestlers he ever tutored." In another, "he was considered by his coach Ed Gallagher as one of the most resourceful and wise wrestlers he ever coached."

Pat was thought so highly of by Gallagher that many expected he would be the successor to the A&M throne when Gallagher was ready to step down. *The Manhattan Mercury* reported on May 5, 1938,

> Patterson is No. 1 man for the A. and M. job when it breaks. Pat is one of the best liked coaches in the Wildcat athletic department and has brought Kansas State's wrestling teams into prominence by arranging attractive home schedules putting scrapping teams on the mat to pack in crowds which rival basketball turnouts.

Patterson as coach of the University of Illinois. He spent twenty years at K-State, three at the University of Nebraska, and eighteen at Illinois before retiring in 1968.
Photo Credit: University of Illinois Archives.

Gallagher's admiration for his pupil may have been rooted in the pupil's style, which reflected the mentor. Accounts of Gallagher's calm demeanor and technical proficiency are strikingly similar to reports of Patterson's style.

When he passed away in 1940, Art Griffith, not Patterson, succeeded Gallagher. Griffith came to A&M from Central High School in Tulsa, where he guided the Braves to ten Oklahoma High School state titles and two high school national titles. Under his leadership, A&M continued its winning ways, accumulating eight NCAA titles in his thirteen years with the Pokes.

It would have been interesting to see if A&M would have had similar success under Patterson—and if K-State would have continued to rise had he remained in Manhattan rather than making the move to the University of Nebraska.

Patterson was inducted into the Helms Foundation Amateur Wrestling Hall of Fame in 1959[3] and the Illinois Wrestling Coaches and Officials Association Hall of Fame in 1974. In the fall of 2024, he was inducted into the Kansas Wrestling Coaches Association Hall of Fame.

Patterson's time as the school's boxing coach was an interesting wrinkle. There is no indication that he had previous experience in the sport either as a competitor or coach.

Several wrestlers participated in both sports. A couple of the more notable crossovers included future K-State head coach and All-American wrestler Leon "Red" Reynard and John Crawley, who was a guard on the football team, wrestler, and captain-elect of the 1936-37 boxing team.

The 1934 *Royal Purple* yearbook notes that Patterson had been the wrestling coach for six years, and with the "revival of inner-collegiate boxing, he has taken over the job of boxing mentor."[4] Boxing lasted only two seasons, 1934-35 and 1935-36, but K-State did participate in the 1936 national championships, held at the University of Virginia, where Patterson coached four individuals. The Cats scored just a single team point.

The most successful boxer in the short-lived history of the K-State program was lightweight R.V. "Bus" Breese from Leonardville. He won local and regional competitions and qualified for the National Collegiate Olympic Boxing Tryouts, held April 8-9, 1932, in State College, Pennsylvania. Breese traveled to Pennsylvania without a coach, sponsor, or teammates. He was eliminated in the second round.

The origins of boxing were similar to wrestling at K-State, where the intramural program was used to test its popularity. From there, an exhibition with KU was held in March of 1925,[5] but until Patterson's hire, it did not get off the ground as a varsity sport for another seven years. After only two seasons of competition, a simple headline of "Boxing dropped at K.S.C."[6] announced the program's demise. The article cited the need for more scheduling support from the Big Six and the difficulty of finding suitable opponents outside the conference.

Back row: Coach Patterson. McDonald. Pyles
Front row: Hund, Madison, Crawley, Stephens

1936 K-State Boxing team led by Coach Patterson. The university sponsored a varsity boxing team from 1934-36. Prior, the sport was offered within its intramural program.
Photo Credit: Collegiate Media Group.

The funding and scheduling issues were too much to overcome, but K-State had the personnel in place. Patterson was a proven coach, and Athletic Director Mike Ahearn was a leader in the sport. Boxing was among the many sports he participated in during his youth, and he was Chairman of the Kansas State Athletic Commission, which supervised both amateur and professional wrestling and boxing. Previously, he served on the National Boxing Commission.

The NCAA continuously held a boxing national championship from 1936-60 but discontinued it in 1961.[7]

When "Pat" moved on to Nebraska in 1947, the wrestling program was on solid enough footing to have the ability to make a big hire without going outside of the program.

Leon "Red" Reynard was born in Burr Oak, Kansas, but moved to Texas shortly after and graduated from Pharr San Juan Alamo High School in San Juan, Texas in 1931. He immediately enlisted in the

U.S. Navy after graduation, where he served for four years before enrolling at Kansas State.

He stood out for the Wildcats on both the wrestling and football teams. He captured three Big Six titles on the mat and capped his career off with a third-place finish in the 1940 NCAAs at 175 pounds.

Reynard had success as K-State's skipper and the program continued to move in the right direction, but after six years, the father of six sought employment as a car salesman at Stubblefield in Manhattan, where he sold Lincolns.

In 1956, Red and his wife, Martha, opened Reynard's Chuckwagon Cafe in Manhattan. Later, the name was changed to Reynard's Restaurant, and the establishment moved from 220 North Main to 622 Tuttle Creek Boulevard. They also operated Reynard's Coffee Shop out of the Wareham Hotel in Manhattan.

Coach Buel "Pat" Patterson reaches over the ring to shake hands with NCAA All-American and future Kansas State head coach, Leon "Red" Reynard during the 1939-40 season. This was the last season wrestling matches were contested in a boxing-style ring at K-State.
Photo credit: Collegiate Media Group

The Fritz Knorr-era was ushered in after Reynard's departure. Knorr was on the wrestling roster in the late 1920s-early 30s but had trouble breaking into the lineup, given the powerful teams of that era.

As a senior, he was beaten out for a spot in the lineup but was thought highly enough by Coach Patterson that he was given the responsibility of coaching the freshman team. He was brought on as head coach to lead the team after Reynard's departure, but this wasn't his first time being part of the Wildcat wrestling program.

When Coach Patterson was deployed to Germany during WWII, Knorr was sought out to fulfill the duties of the wrestling coach. No wrestling competitions were held from 1942-46, and Patterson was still the coach of record, but Knorr was appointed to keep the program going until its post-war reinstatement and Patterson's return from deployment in Europe.

A dual meet against Ft. Hays State University was held in an auxiliary gym in Ahearn Fieldhouse on Saturday, December 14, 1957. K-State won 22-7 in the season-opener for both teams. On the mat is K-State's Pat Doyle (left) and Claran Voss in the 157-pound match. Doyle, the defending Big Seven Champion, won 5-0. He is the son of K-State's 1931 NCAA Champion, Bill Doyle, the first native Kansan to win an NCAA wrestling title and the only one to do so while representing a Kansas school.
Photo Credit: Collegiate Media Group.

Knorr served in the capacity of head coach from 1953 until his sudden death from a heart attack in September 1972. Maybe the most interesting part of Knorr's tenure is that he was K-State's Basketball Head Coach from 1944-46 and also served as head baseball coach (1949-50) and assistant coach for the football program along the way.

The "Fritz G. Knorr Memorial Athletic Scholarship" (originally earmarked for the wrestling program) is an endowed scholarship that is awarded to a deserving baseball player at K-State to this day.

Knorr continued to develop and promote the sport as his mentor Patterson did. In 1956, he began hosting a coaching clinic that brought in high school coaches from across the state. That clinic has taken place each fall since 1956. After his passing in 1972, his name appeared in the clinic's title that it maintains to this day: the KWCA Fritz Knorr Fall Clinic.

Fritz Knorr's association with K-State began as a student in 1928 and ended forty-four years later with his untimely death in September 1972 after nineteen years as head coach of the wrestling program. Pictured are members of the 1958-59 team (l-r) Don Darter, Pat Doyle, Larry Caster, Jim Caster, and Coach Knorr. *Photo Credit:* Collegiate Media Group.

Like his mentor, Knorr also served on the NCAA Wrestling Rules Committee. He was on the committee for five years and served as chairman during the 1960-61 season when the controversial takedown rule was put in place that lasted for only the 1961-62 season.

The rule, which seemingly was targeted at Oklahoma State, awarded two points for the first takedown in a match, but only a single point for subsequent takedowns. The Cowboys were known as takedown artists, who could run up the score by accumulating takedowns without much focus on attempting to pin their opponents.

Knorr hosted the first Kansas Kid's state tournament at Manhattan

High School in 1964 and continued until 1972. That tournament has been an annual event in Kansas for sixty years and is now one of the nation's largest kid's state tournaments. In 2024, a record 2,446 participants from 187 clubs participated in the three-day event in Topeka.

In 2005, the National Wrestling Hall of Fame posthumously awarded Knorr its Lifetime Service Award.

With only weeks until the start of the 1972-73 season, Dale Samuelson was handed the clipboard and whistle, going from graduate assistant one day to head coach the next after Knorr's passing. Upon completion of the season, a search for a permanent head coach was conducted. Out of the running, Samuelson returned to his Northwest Kansas roots, where he had a long and productive career as a teacher and coach at Oakley High School. In his first year at his alma mater, the Plainsmen won the 1974 State Championship in Class 2-1A.

If not for the whistle around his neck, 22 year-old head coach Dale Samuelson (front row, far left) would appear to be a member of the team in the 1972-73 team picture. Top row: Roger Fisher, David Spear, Joe Creedon, Wayne Jackson, Mark Jackson, Gregg Barnes, Steve Hale, Jeff Stafford. Second row: Phil Martin, Pat Debold, Mike Brungardt, Roger Washburn, Dan Ruda, Jim Lundberg, Sig White. Third row: Eric Hilding, Fred Foos, Gary Walter, Phil Donley, Dan Keller, Paul Nelson. Bottom row: Dale Samuelson (Head Coach), Steve Scannell, Chuck Merritt, Tony Harris, Dan Rogers, Dick Keller, Rick Taylor
Photo Credit: Collegian Media Group.

Fred Fozzard became the last coach in Kansas State wrestling history when he was hired after a national search. His tenure was short-lived, lasting only two years (1973-75). As NCAA and World Champion, Fozzard had the credentials as a competitor and was on staff at Oklahoma State University. That combination made him as high-profile a candidate as anyone in the market.

Coming in, Fozzard was enthused and eager to bring the Wildcats to relevance in the rugged Big Eight Conference and on the national stage. "We're going to have a real program here," Fozzard said in a *Kansas State Collegian* article shortly after arriving on campus in July 1973. He went on to say, "I know it can't be done all at once, but I'm confident I can do it. I'm impatient and can't wait to get it going."

The Fozzard years, however, were marked by communication problems with Athletic Director Ernie Barrett and financial struggles for the entire athletic department. Fozzard was fired in April 1975, and the program was officially dropped three months later.

Fred Fozzard was the last coach in K-State wrestling history, leading the Cats
for the 1973-74 and 1974-75 seasons. The NCAA and World Champion
was previously an assistant at Oklahoma State University, his alma mater.
Photo Credit: Oklahoma State University Archives.

After Fozzard was dismissed, there is no evidence that the athletic department was interested in continuing the program. An interim coach was not named, nor was there an indication of a national search for Fozzard's replacement. The announcement in July was little more than confirmation of what was already apparent: K-State would no longer be supporting a wrestling program.

With your appetite whetted, let's dig a little deeper and look at some of the more interesting personalities and intriguing aspects of Kansas State University Wildcat Wrestling and its wider impact on the sport in the state of Kansas.

Chapter One Endnotes: *A Brief History*

1. For consistency, this book will use "K-State," "Kansas State," and "Kansas State University" throughout to represent the name of the current Kansas State University regardless of era.
2. The Normal College of Physical Education of Indianapolis began an affiliation with Indiana University in 1932.
3. The Helms Foundation Amateur Wrestling Hall of Fame's charter class was inducted in 1957. That group of six included Ed Gallagher. Patterson was inducted in the next class, 1959. The Helms Foundation began instituting halls of fame for various sports in 1936 and continued until the early 1980s when individual sports had established their own halls of fame. The LA84 Foundation absorbed the Helms collection and now manages its databases and physical artifacts.
4. "Buel R. Patterson has been wrestling coach at Kansas State for six years and this year with the revival of inner-collegiate boxing he has taken over the job of boxing mentor." 1934 *Royal Purple*, p. 145.
5. Ray Pyles (118 pounds), Russell Madiso (135 pounds, team captain), Frank Hund (165 pounds), and John Crawley (175 pounds).
6. "Boxing Dropped at KSU" *The Morning Chronicle* (Manhattan) Tuesday, November 3, 1936.
7. For more on the history of collegiate boxing and perennial power of University of Wisconsin's program, *Lords of the Ring: The Triumph and Tragedy of College Boxing's Greatest Team* by Doug Moe, is an interesting read.

-2-
Bill Doyle, First and Only

The story of the first and only Kansan to win an NCAA DI wrestling championship while representing a Kansas school is as compelling as it is unique.[1] It is a story rooted in the very foundation of the movement to sanction high school wrestling in the state of Kansas and part of the era that produced the most successful team in the history of college wrestling in Kansas.

Bill Doyle arrived on the K-State campus in the fall of 1926 from Douglass, a rough-and-tumble oil town in southeast Kansas with a declining population of 804, according to the 1930 census. Located about a half-hour drive to the Oklahoma border, or twenty miles southeast of Wichita, the town is one of the original hotbeds of wrestling in Kansas, and Bill Doyle can take part of the credit for that.

Bill Doyle made history in 1930 when he coached Douglass to the first state wrestling championship in Kansas history. A year later, he again made history by winning the NCAA title in the 145-pound weight class for Kansas State University.
Photo Credit: Collegian Media Group.

Doyle had never competed in a regulation wrestling match before enrolling at K-State. He came to the school on a baseball scholarship, which in that day meant he was given a job on campus to help with college expenses. When the school's wrestling coach, Buel "Pat" Patterson, saw the strapping lad around the playing fields, he persuaded him to give wrestling a try. Doyle quickly took to the new sport, becoming intramural champion at a time when freshmen could not participate on the varsity team. Wrestling became his focus, with baseball lasting only through his freshman season.

John (Pat) Doyle followed in his father's footsteps by becoming a standout wrestler at K-State. *Photo Credit*: Collegian Media Group.

Part of the fascination with the sport came from Coach Patterson's coaching style. He was positive and encouraging, with a work ethic like no other. He was the type of coach who commanded rather than demanded respect; his wrestlers would run through a brick wall for him. Doyle meshed with Pat, and the coach saw something in the pupil that manifested itself as unprecedented success on the mat.

Doyle thought so highly of Coach Patterson, even long after his college days were behind him, that he named his son after him. John Patrick Doyle, born March 23, 1937, in Salina, would follow in his father's footsteps and compete for the Wildcats, winning a Big Seven Championship in 1957 and qualifying for the NCAAs in 1957 and 1958. Many in the family did not know, but "John" came from Doyle's best friend and teammate at K-State, John Richardson, and Patrick from Coach Patterson's nickname, "Pat." The family has a John and Patrick in its lineage, so that was the presumed origin of the name. The younger Doyle, who currently lives in the Minneapolis/St. Paul metro, has gone by his middle name his entire life.

Interestingly, Doyle's other child, Sally, four years older than her brother, married Thane Baker, the most decorated Olympic track and field athlete in K-State history. He won a silver medal in the 200 meters in Helsinki in 1952 and a gold, silver, and bronze in Melbourne in 1956. Married in 1954, Sally was in Melbourne to support her husband's historic performance. She passed away in 2021. The couple was married for sixty-six years.

After two years of toiling away in the classroom and on the mat, Doyle and Richardson dropped out of college and moved to southeast Kansas to work in the oil fields around Douglass. The plan, however, took an unexpected turn. Shortly after arriving, Doyle was approached about taking on a teacher/coach role at Douglass High School.

In the fall of 1923, it was announced that DHS had started a wrestling program. Head football and basketball coach Clarence Little organized the effort, and Alvin "Guy" Elliott was charged with the coaching duties, a position he held through the start-up and for the first year, 1927-28, when the Bulldogs competed through their first official schedule of competitions.

Elliott hailed from the central Iowa community of Collins, where he gained notoriety in professional wrestling circles. After moving to Kansas, where relatives lived, he married Harriett Fox, a Douglass local. When they relocated to her Oklahoma roots, an opening was created in the upstart Bulldog wrestling program.

Richardson remained in the oil fields, but it was an offer Doyle couldn't refuse. He taught shop classes and became the head wrestling coach at Douglass for two seasons, 1928-30.

The sport of wrestling was not only growing in popularity at the collegiate level in the early 1900s, interest was also growing in high schools across the state. In 1928 and 1929, Coach Patterson organized a high school invitational tournament and held it in Manhattan. In 1928 it was hosted at Manhattan High School. The next year, the event was hosted at Nichols Hall on the K-State campus.

Patterson worked hard to develop wrestling at the grass-roots level in Kansas. He believed it was essential to be more competitive at the college level. An article in the *Manhattan Mercury* dated March

4, 1930, reported:

> Coach Patterson came from Oklahoma, where
> wrestling has been an outstanding sport in high schools
> for 20 years and realizes that Kansas colleges and
> universities will be unable to compete with the
> Oklahoma institutions until wrestlers are developed
> early. And he says the time for them to learn the
> fundamentals is when they are in high school.

By 1930, with the state high school athletic association's approval, the invitational had grown into the first sanctioned high school state wrestling tournament in Kansas history. The following ten teams[2] gathered at Nichols Hall on Friday, February 28th for a two-day tournament to determine state-wide honors: Clay Center (Coach Zurlinder Pearson), Columbus (Coach Paul Hawkins), Douglass (Coach Bill Doyle), Hoxie (Coach A.B. Keith), Hutchinson (Coach J. Earl Taylor), Kinsley (Coach L.T. Workman),[3] Oberlin (Coach Lester Kirkendall), Salina (Coach N.A.B. Huckelby), Wichita East (Coach Cornelia), and Kansas City-Wyandotte (Coach Roy). Competitors filled the following nine weight classes: 95, 105, 115, 125, 135, 145, 155, 165, and Unlimited.

Like today's state-level events sponsored by the Kansas State High School Activities Association (KSHSAA), school activity passes were not honored. Admission for each session was 25 cents. An all-session pass was priced at 50 cents.

Wichita High (renamed Wichita East before the 1929-30 school year when Wichita North opened) won the invitational in 1928 and 1929, with Douglass taking runner-up honors in '29 during Doyle's first year at Douglass. It is interesting to note that Pittsburg State University lost out but was also vying to host the first official state meet. PSU held invitationals in 1928 and 1929, and they were also monitored by the state's high school athletic association under the direction of Caleb W. Smick, Decatur county superintendent of schools and state high school athletic commission board member, and board secretary E.A. Thomas. The "Interstate Wrestling Invitational" was held on the campus of Pittsburg Teachers College and involved teams from Kansas, Missouri, and Oklahoma.

Interestingly, Patterson's college teammate and Alpha Gamma Rho fraternity brother at A&M, Leon Bauman, who was then coaching at Kansas University, also wanted to be in the mix to host the high school state tournament.

Buel "Pat" Patterson coached the 1931 Kansas State University Wildcats to a third-place finish in the NCAA tournament. Doyle thought so highly of Patterson that he named his son after him. *Photo Credit*: Collegian Media Group.

Pat served as referee for the KU vs. Nebraska dual around the time the athletic commission was making the host site decision. Before the competition began, the two agreed that the winner of a coin flip would host the first high school state tournament and subsequent tournaments would alternate between the two schools going forward. There is no indication that Bauman and KU were as serious about hosting events and involvement in wrestling's grassroots development like Pat was, but the exchange was interesting enough to make its way into a newspaper article.[4]

Going into the 1930 tournament, prognosticators put the field on notice that Douglass was the odds-on favorite to ink its name as the historic first state wrestling champion. The team put together an impressive season against the Kansas competition and even the more established programs from Oklahoma.

When the dust settled, Douglass came away with a commanding victory. The Bulldogs accumulated 32 points, twelve more than Wichita East, the runner-up. Douglass had a trio of individual state champions: Alvin Darter (115 pounds), Lawrence Cox (125 pounds), and Wilfred Darter (145 pounds). Pete Mehringer, who would win Olympic Gold in Los Angeles only two years later, was champion at heavyweight for Kinsley High School. He hitchhiked the two hundred miles from the southwest Kansas community and reportedly competed without a coach in his corner.

Bill Doyle had other interests besides wrestling. He was smitten when he met a young lady from Rock, Kansas, named Alberta Hornaday. Bill asked Alberta on a double date. A friend, possibly John Richardson, borrowed a car, which might have been a Model A Ford. Bill and Alberta rode in the rumble seat from Rock to Wichita and back on gravel roads. They became close.

Bill Doyle was not only a successful wrestler and wrestling coach, he was also a formidable football and track and field coach. *Photo Credit*: Catherine Baker Nicholson collection.

So, there you have it. Native son Bill Doyle returns to his hometown after a stint in college and rides off into the sunset with the first state title in Kansas history. Only Doyle was not done writing the script.

Richardson made the trip back to Manhattan for the high school championships to support his friend's quest to make history. Coach Patterson was the tournament manager and had his team on hand to help run the event. Maybe it was a nudge from Coach Pat, or maybe it was being in the arena and getting the chance to catch up with former teammates. Whatever transpired, both committed to returning to K-State to finish school and use the remainder of their eligibility on the mat. Doyle resigned at Douglass High, pulled his friend out of the oil field, and the pair headed back to Manhattan.

In their absence, Coach Patterson continued to build the program. The Wildcats were becoming formidable opponents even to the most seasoned teams. With the addition of Doyle and Richardson, the team would have the firepower to compete against anyone. And compete they did!

The 1931 squad claimed the Big Six championship with victories over powerhouses like Iowa State and Oklahoma. It is important to note that Oklahoma A&M was not part of the Big Six, which was formed in 1928. The Cowboys did not enter the conference until 1958, when it had expanded to become the Big Eight. This perspective is important because a victory at the time over Oklahoma A&M would have been shocking. The Pokes were a dynasty under Ed Gallagher. In 1931, they were the three-time defending NCAA champions and would also win it in dominating fashion that year.

Brown University in Providence, Rhode Island, hosted the 1931 NCAA tournament on March 27-28. Coach Patterson drove four Kansas State athletes to the East Coast for the event and put together a tournament that would never be matched again.

Joe Fickel (Chanute) placed third at 126 pounds. Hugh Errington (Ruleton/Goodland), K-State's first All-American in 1930, matched his placing of a year earlier with a third place showing at heavyweight. Richardson (Dodge City) finished as NCAA runner-up at 155 pounds after spending the previous two years working the oil fields of southeast Kansas. Leathered and tough as nails, Richardson had a successful run on the professional wrestling scene in the Midwest after his college days.

And then there was Richardson's friend, Bill Doyle. The previous March, he coached tiny Douglass High to the first state championship in Kansas history. One year later, he was busy claiming the biggest prize in college wrestling, the NCAA championship! Doyle defeated Walter Young of Oklahoma A&M in the 145-pound final after earlier victories over Syracuse, Iowa State, and Tufts opponents. This was the first NCAA wrestling title for a native Kansan and remains the only NCAA D1 title for a wrestler representing a Kansas college or university.

At the time, All-American status was awarded to only the top three in each weight class.[5] The four All-Americans for the Cats would finish behind only champion Oklahoma A&M and runner-up Iowa State. Iowa Teachers (now the University of Northern Iowa) was fourth, and Lehigh rounded out the top five.

Doyle returned to Douglass and married Alberta on July 1, 1930, in the parsonage of the Methodist Church in Douglass. The couple returned to Manhattan that fall.

In Manhattan, besides going to school and training, Bill and Alberta ran the bus station in town. Alberta already had her teaching degree from Emporia State, but Bill had one more year to finish his degree.

Doyle was looking to defend his NCAA title in 1932 at Indiana University, but a late-season illness slowed him, and he took a few uncharacteristic losses. He visited a physician who immediately hospitalized the weakened champion and diagnosed him with Typhoid Fever. He was failing. At the most critical point, he was down to ninety pounds. Days before the team left for the NCAA Championships, John Richardson carried him out of the hospital, and Coach Patterson carried him up three flights of stairs to the apartment Doyle shared with his wife. Eventually, he made a full recovery.

With his collegiate career behind him, his focus eventually returned to coaching at the high school level, but before that, he sampled other career options. Doyle also continued to wrestle as a post-collegiate and attempted to make the 1936 Olympic team in the 145.5-pound weight class. He won the Missouri Valley regional qualifier and the National YMCA tournament at Wilkes-Barre, Pennsylvania, one of three Olympic Trials semi-final events. It was reported that Coach Patterson accompanied him to the final round of trials at Lehigh University, but Doyle does not appear in the summary of results.

The bus company in Manhattan transferred the Doyles to Salina, Kansas. Later, they operated the Old English Grille, a restaurant downtown. In Salina, they had their children, Sally Jeanette in 1933, and John Patrick, four years later. From Salina, they moved to a farm outside Norton, Kansas, where Doyle worked for the government appraising farms. They also raised sheep and horses.

After the government job in Norton ended, Alberta's brother, Otis Hornaday, persuaded the Doyles to move to southern California. Hornaday was superintendent of schools in what is now the Palo Verde Unified School District in Blythe, California. He hired Doyle to teach physical education and take on head coaching duties in wrestling and football at Palo Verde Union High School. Every summer the family, with their Airedale Terrier, Ted, drove back to Kansas in their car without air conditioning and lived with Alberta's parents.

Doyle found success in Blythe, including coaching the football team to a Tri-Valley League runner-up finish in 1949, but a contract dispute and unmet promises from the new superintendent soured him on putting down roots. After three years in California, the 1949-50 school year would be the last in the Golden State.

He was enticed to move back to Douglass, where he re-established the wrestling program that had been dormant since 1939.

Coach Patterson had moved on from his position at K-State and was head coach at the University of Nebraska. Doyle's move back to Kansas coincided with Pat's next move to the University of Illinois. Nebraska Athletic Director George "Potsy" Clark contacted Doyle about taking the position vacated by Patterson, but Doyle felt that he had to honor his commitment to Douglass and turned the offer down.

During his return to Douglass High, Doyle had a solid six years as head coach of the reinstated wrestling program. He built it back to state-contender status. In his first two seasons, the Bulldogs didn't score a point at the state tournament. During his final four seasons, the team finished in the top ten each year, including a pair of fourth-place finishes.

He also served as head coach of the reinstated Bulldog football program, where he found similar success as he did on the mat. The state playoff system for football did not start in Kansas until 1969; thus, statewide accomplishments weren't part of that sport's landscape during Doyle's era. Douglass went 8-1 in 1953, 7-1 in 1955, and 8-0 in 1956 with Doyle at the helm.

The Bulldog wrestling program would win the state championship for the second time in school history in 1960 under Doyle's successor, Darrell Hill. Hill, who also took over head football coaching duties, was an outstanding tackle for the University of Wichita football team and was the 1951 state champion at heavyweight for Topeka High.

Coach Doyle's impact on the wrestling landscape can't be understated, but his impact on track and field is also impressive.

From 1955 until 1975, the state of Kansas held an indoor state track and field championship. Like wrestling in 1930, Douglass was the first high school to win the Kansas State Indoor Track and Field competition.[6] And like wrestling in 1930, Bill Doyle was the head coach of the 1955 Douglass Bulldog team! Ironically, the first indoor championship was hosted on the K-State campus as was wrestling in 1930. Wrestling was held in Nichols Hall, and track and field at Ahearn Field House. Doyle also led Douglass to the 1956 and 1957 indoor titles and the 1956 and 1957 Outdoor State Championships in Class B.

Doyle left Douglass High in 1957, where he also taught math and science, to take over a similar teaching and coaching role at a new all-boys school in Wichita, Chaplain Kapaun Memorial High School, which later became the current co-ed Kapaun Mt. Carmel Catholic High School.[7]

Doyle served as the first wrestling coach at Kapaun when the sport was established in the fall of 1957. It was reported by the *Wichita Evening Eagle* on November 26, 1957, that: "In its first year of wrestling competition, Emil Kapaun Memorial High School has a turnout of nearly 100 prospective grapplers. The school's total enrollment is only 575 boys."

The program was headed in the right direction, but fate would intervene before his new school would see the full impact of Coach Doyle. He died of a heart attack on April 23, 1960, while driving to his home in Douglass from his rural property eleven miles east of town. He was just fifty-three years old.

His wife of twenty-eight years, Alberta, daughter, Sally, son, John (Pat), and one-year-old granddaughter, Catherine, survived him.

Bill and Alberta Doyle's daughter, Sally, married Thane Baker, the most decorated Olympic athlete in K-State's track and field history. In the fall of 2023, he was honored with a bronze bust now displayed in K-State's track and field complex. *Photo Credit: Manhattan Mercury.*

Starting in 1961 until the program was cut in 1975, the K-State wrestling program awarded the Bill Doyle Memorial Trophy to its outstanding wrestler. To this day, Kapaun Mt. Carmel Catholic High School awards the Bill Doyle Memorial Award to "an outstanding male athlete who has demonstrated hard work, achievement, and pride during their high school career to excel both academically and athletically."

Doyle was a well-traveled wrestling official, working Big 8 tournaments, NCAA championships, and K-State home duals. He was also selected to officiate at the 1960 Summer Olympics in Rome.

Doyle was inducted into the Kansas Wrestling Coaches Association (KWCA) Hall of Fame in 1982. The Kansas State High School Activities Association (KSHSAA) inducted Doyle into its Hall of Fame in 1990. He was inducted into the Douglass High School Hall of Fame, Class of 2021-2022.

Following his death in 1960, The Bill Doyle Memorial Award was presented to K-State's outstanding wrestler at its banquet. In 1963, head coach Fritz Knorr presented the award to Joe Seay.

"My dad was a good man. He didn't drink. Didn't smoke. He worked hard and treated people right. He was a great wrestler, but he was a great man, too, and I'm fortunate to call him my dad," said his son, Pat, during a 2023 interview from his Shoreview, Minnesota home.

Chapter Two Endnotes: *Bill Doyle, First and Only*

1. The NCAA now has three main divisions: Division I, Division II, and Division III. In 1931 the NCAA had no such divisions. However, to help understand Bill Doyle's achievement from a modern-day perspective, he is referred to as an "NCAA Division I" champion. The DI National Champions from Kansas; Wyatt Hendrickson (2025, 285 pounds) – Oklahoma State University (Newton), Kendric Maple (2013, 141 pounds) – Oklahoma University (Wichita Heights), Zach Roberson (2004, 133 pounds) – Iowa State University (Blue Valley NW), Melvin Douglas (1985 and 1986, 177 pounds) – Oklahoma University (Topeka-Highland Park), Myron Roderick (1954, 137 pounds, 1955 and 1956, 130 pounds) – Oklahoma State University (Winfield), Dale Scrivens (1938, 155 pounds) – Oklahoma State University (Wellington), Bill Doyle (1931, 145 pounds) – Kansas State University (Douglass).

2. Burr Oak, Manhattan, El Dorado, Goodland, and Norton were also listed preliminarily as possible entries, but none of that group participated in the inaugural event.

3. It has been a long-held belief (and even reported in a *Manhattan Mercury* article from March 4, 1930) that 1930 heavyweight state champion and 1932 Olympic Champion Peter Mehringer hitchhiked to the 1930 state tournament and competed without a coach. Whether Coach Workman was a "coach of record" or an actual coach in the corner is lost to history.

4. *The Manhattan Mercury* (Manhattan, Kansas) Monday, February 18, 1929.

5. From 1928-40, the top three earned All-American status, 1941-62, the top four earned All-American status, 1963-78, the top six earned All-American status, and 1979-present, the top eight earn All-American status.

6. Douglass won the state title in Class B. Lawrence-Haskell won the Class A title and Shawnee Mission won the Class AA title.

7. The school is named after Father Emil J. Kapaun. The Medal of Honor recipient served with distinction during the Korean War. Duwane Miller, 1961 NCAA Champion for Oklahoma University, coached at Douglass before two stints at Kapaun. He is one of the all-time coaching greats in Kansas with eight state championships and the only two Grand State championships in Kansas history.

-3-
One Man Gang

In 1864, a fifteen-year-old named James Barton Hackney of Zanesville, Ohio, enlisted in the Union Army during the Civil War as a drummer boy. After a year of service with Company K, 122nd Ohio Volunteer Infantry, he was captured by the Confederate Army and spent thirteen months in Libby Prison in Richmond, Virginia and Andersonville in Georgia. After being honorably discharged, he returned home to Ohio.

At nineteen, his father, George, passed away. James and his family left Zanesville behind and ventured west to start a new life in Atlantic, Iowa, where George had purchased land before his death.

James later separated from the family to set out on his own. He settled on land one-hundred-forty miles west, near the eastern Nebraska community of Seward, under the Soldier's Homestead Act.[1] In 1876 he married a local, Frances Neels.[2] She was eighteen; he was ten years her senior. Three years later, the couple moved two hundred fifty miles southwest to Decatur county in Kansas, enticed by land offered through the U.S. Land Office at Oberlin, a town of about 1,200 residents at the time, located in the far reaches of northwest Kansas. The couple would raise their eight children there.

The farmstead was situated southwest of Oberlin in Bassettville Township on land known as the Laing claim. Just a year before the Hackneys settled there, northern Cheyenne Indians killed five members of the Laing and Westphalian families on the property.

Plat maps from 1905 show that James Hackney owned over 400 acres in Decatur County. He sold part of this land and purchased more in Rawlins County, adjacent to Decatur County to the west. A 1902 newspaper account in the *Oberlin Times* on February 28, 1902, stated, "James Hackney, who lives partly in Decatur and partly in Rawlins county, went to Atwood, Saturday last, to buy more land. Jim is an early settler, has worked hard and become rich."

It is unclear If he was able to maintain the reported wealth. In reviewing later plat maps and ownership logs, it appears that more land was purchased but divided further amongst family members. What is clear is that James and Frances braved the hardships of pioneer life and lived on the property for fifty-three years until his death in September 1932. By then, his son Phillip had assumed ownership of the farm and was caring for his parents. His mother had been an invalid for years.

While working the farm, Phillip was also chief of police in Oberlin. He ran for Decatur County Sheriff in 1932 but was defeated.

Phillip and his wife, Laura, raised their nine children on the farmstead where his father and mother settled. Son Elmer would become a star athlete for the Kansas State Wildcats.

Elmer Loyd Hackney was born on July 8, 1916, in the family's sod house.[3] Vada, the oldest, married Earl Scott of Oberlin at seventeen. Herman was two years older than Elmer, who was the third born. Next came triplets Agnes, Alice, and Anna. They were four years younger than Elmer. Gerald followed in Elmer's footsteps and became a formidable athlete in his own right, first at Decatur Community High School, then at K-State.[4] He was ten years younger than Elmer. Peggy, the youngest, was born in 1931; she followed Lois.

For a period of time in the late 1920s to early 1930s, the number of boarders in Phillip and Laura's household swelled. In addition to Phillip's parents, his oldest brother George also lived with the family. When tragedy struck, they found room for four more.

After Phillip's brother William's sudden death in April 1928, his wife Hattie and their children Kermit, Francis, and Dale also lived with the family. Times were not easy for the Hackneys.

Joseph and Hilda Perrill also raised a large family on farms in northwest Kansas. They first lived in Allison (Decatur County) and Lenora (Norton County) before relocating to the community of Norton; thirty miles from Oberlin, directly east on 36 Highway. The couple, sixteen years apart, had eight children. Erma, the oldest, was born in 1914. Another sibling followed her about every two years until Gladys arrived in 1930.

Ellen was the second oldest of the five girls and three boys. She did not attend high school, going through the eighth grade during her formative years.

Ellen Perrill and Elmer Hackney met at a social function sometime in their early teens. They became a couple and were married in a double wedding ceremony on July 19, 1936, in her home in Norton. The other couple was Elmer's brother Herman who married Ellen's sister, Erma. Elmer was just two months separated from his high school graduation and the same distance away from setting foot on the Kansas State University campus.

Elmer and Ellen were married in a double wedding on July 19, 1936, at the home of Ellen's parents, Joseph and Hilda Perrill in Norton. The other couple was Elmer's brother, Herman, and Ellen's sister, Erma. Elmer would begin at K-State two months later. *Photo Credit*: Jamie Garten collection.

It is unclear when and how Elmer was introduced to athletics, but his work ethic and engagement in manual labor that was part of daily life on the farm certainly contributed to what he was to become on the playing fields. Hackney is still considered one of the greatest multisport athletes in K-State history.

Despite being slowed by injuries late in his career, Elmer Hackney still had the accolades and recognition to be revered as one of the greatest all-around athletes in K-State history, even over eight decades later. *Photo Credit*: Hearst Holdings, Inc., King Features Syndicate Division.

Before arriving at K-State in the fall of 1936, Elmer had accumulated impressive credentials in high school. In 1933, as a freshman, he finished as state runner-up in wrestling while competing in the heavyweight division. He was state champion as a sophomore and senior and would have likely been the first Kansas four-time state finalist and three-time champion, but the tournament was canceled in 1935 due to not enough schools being committed to fielding wrestling teams.[5]

Hackney did not have the opportunity to defend his state title in 1935, but he did participate in the Missouri Valley A.A.U. tournament held at K-State[6] on March 15-16. As a seventeen-year-old, Hackney performed well against college competition. The high school junior placed second to Clyde "Tiny" Moore of the University of Kansas. Reports of the mammoth heavyweight have him listed at 6' 4" and weighing between 275 – 300 pounds. Moore, who won the Big Six title only the weekend prior, also played football for KU. Hackney dropped a 10-2 decision to the seasoned collegiate but won by fall over current K-State wrestler, Rolla Holland, to claim runner-up honors. Earlier in the tournament, Holland had nearly pinned Moore twice before succumbing to the massive Jayhawk.

The tournament drew select high school wrestlers, wrestlers on college rosters, and even post-grads who were pursuing Olympic dreams. The 1935 tournament field included current K-State stars Ernest Jessup and Forrest Fansher. Also making the walk were alumnus June Roberts and Bill Doyle.

Hackney won a Big Six championship at heavyweight in 1938 and helped draw record crowds to Nichols Hall for dual meets. *Photo Credit*: Collegian Media Group

Hackney also excelled on the gridiron and as a shot putter on the track and field team at Decatur Community High School, but not to the level of his wrestling prowess. No one could have predicted the success that would come in college.

In reflecting on his career after announcing his retirement, legendary Kansas State Track and Field coach Ward Haylett used Hackney as an example. "The biggest thrill in coaching, to me, is taking a kid with just an average amount of ability and helping him develop." As an example of this synthesis, Haylett points to Elmer Hackney. As reported by *The Manhattan Mercury* on April 19, 1961, "Hackney, shot putter here in the late 1930s, was not a standout in high school, but left K-State holding the national collegiate record for the event." Hackney never even qualified for state in the shot during his time at Oberlin High.

It didn't take long for the moniker "One Man Gang" to be attached to him for his bruising play on the football field. Once he padded up for the Cats, he quickly rose in the ranks and was a bona fide star before the end of his sophomore season.

Hackney was a punishing fullback, busting through the line to clear the way and often bringing two or three would-be tacklers with him when he carried the pigskin. The All-Big Six selection as a junior was tabbed a pre-season All-American before his senior campaign, but an injury in the opener against Ft. Hays State kept him sidelined for several games and he was less effective for the remainder of the season when he was cleared to be back on the field.

Opponents ran scout team simulations to prepare specifically for Hackney. "When One Man Gang Elmer Hackney tucks the ball away and starts out, defensive men just grit their teeth and prepare for the worst. Hackney, who weighs no less than 200 pounds, packs more power than any other man on the squad."[7]

"They watched Elmer Hackney, famed as the One Man Gang, demonstrate why they refer to him as the individual riot. No bull in a china shop ever caused more confusion than those bustling blasts that this 205-pounder from Oberlin, Kansas puts on as he roared through the Husker line."[8] The game that generated that quote in 1938, played against Nebraska in Lincoln, elicited an ovation from the Husker crowd. "Hackney carried three tacklers with him on a 16-yard romp which netted Kansas State a touchdown. The K-State fullback received a tremendous ovation from the holiday crowd of 22,000 when he was taken out a few plays later."[9] "We have a lot of respect for this fellow Hackney,"[10] said Nebraska coach Biff Jones.

Despite the truncated senior campaign, the Philadelphia Eagles drafted him in the 11th round (92nd overall pick) of the 1940 NFL draft. He played in Philly for a season and then for the Steelers for a year. Hackney spent the next five seasons as a Detroit Lion before concluding his seven-year stint in the NFL in 1946. He ended his pro career with twelve touchdowns and 846 rushing yards. He started fourteen games and maintained his bruising reputation from his college days.

Elmer Hackney (41) talks with teammate Davey O'Brien while the two played for the Philadelphia Eagles. O'Brien was the first Southeast Conference player to win the Heisman Trophy during his college days at TCU.
Photo Credit: Jamie Garten collection

During Hackney's 1940 season in Philly, he had the unique experience of playing in two games against the Brooklyn Dodgers. It wasn't playing in the games that was unique. It was who was wearing #10 for the opposition.

Sam Francis graduated from Decatur Community High School in 1933 when Hackney was a freshman. Francis was a high school champion shot putter and accomplished on the gridiron. After spending a short time on the University of Kansas campus, he enrolled at the University of Nebraska, where he excelled in both sports.

Francis was runner-up to Yale's Larry Kelley in the 1937 Heisman trophy voting and was the overall first pick of the 1937 NFL Draft. He also won the 1937 NCAA shot put title after making the 1936 U.S. Olympic team and placing fourth at the Berlin Olympics. Elmer Hackney is considered by many to be the greatest athlete in the history of K-State but has stiff competition for the same title in Oberlin, Kansas!

Hackney was motivated by the accolades and notoriety that Francis gained throughout his college career. During his string of record-breaking shot-put throws during his junior season, one that he prized most was the toss of 52' 1½" in April of 1939 at the KU Relays. That throw eclipsed the previous meet record by 7.5 inches, a record set by Nebraska's Sam Francis.

The two titans from rural northwest Kansas, now with the NFL, played against each other on October 4 at Ebbets Field in New York when the Brooklyn Dodgers hosted the Philadelphia Eagles and again on October 26 at Philadelphia's Shibe Park. Although the stats were not impressive for either in those games (Hackney scored a touchdown in the first game), it is most impressive that two athletes of that caliber came from rural northwest Kansas and displayed their talents at the highest levels of professional sports.

Ellen and Elmer holding twins Judy and Trudy. Standing is Betty. The picture was taken in 1948. Photo Credit: Jamie Garten collection.

In September 1940, President Franklin D. Roosevelt signed into law the Selective Training and Service Act, also known simply as The Draft. In 1941, after the Japanese bombing on December 7, 1941, of Pearl Harbor, Congress amended the act to require all able-bodied men ages 18 to 64 to register with their local draft board for military service for the duration of World War II plus six months after. This time period coincided with the prime of Hackney's football career.

In December of 1943, Elmer reported for his physical at Fort Leavenworth during his time with the Detroit Lions. Due to his injured knee, he did not pass the physical and was rejected for military service. Elmer did, however, contribute to the cause of the war by helping construct an airbase in Casper, Wyoming, and other war-related construction projects in Nebraska.

As strange as it seems, Hackney failed the military's physical standard but was able to play another three seasons in the NFL. And play he did!

The 1945 Detroit Lions. Elmer Hackney is in the back row, fourth from the right (#34). This Lions team finished second in the NFL Western Division with a 7-3 record. The head coach was Gus Dorais (pictured top row, far left). *Photo Credit*: Jamie Garten Collection.

A Detroit Lions publicity release from 1946 had high praise for the utility player. "Hackney has been a valuable asset to the Lions both on offense and defense. His line smashes, with knees pumping high, have accounted for many a needed yard. Likewise, because of his height and better than average speed, he gives top-flight protection against opponent's passes."

His best game occurred in 1944 against the Boston Yanks.[11] In that game, he scored three touchdowns:

In Sunday's game against the Boston Yanks at Detroit, Hackney scored three of the Lion's five touchdowns, two on four-yard thru-the-line smashes, and the other on an eight-yard pass from Bob Westfall. The one-time Georgia great, Frankie Sinkwich, is also a Lions player, but Hackney gets most of the credit for this year's showing, it seems. The Lions are tied for second in the final western division standings of that league.[12]

Hackney's wrestling success after high school took a backseat to his football and track and field accomplishments. He competed on the wrestling team at K-State for only his first three years, forgoing his senior season to concentrate on healing the injured knee from football. He was the Big Six Champion at heavyweight as a sophomore in 1938 and runner-up as a junior.

Hackney was center stage when the Aggies of Oklahoma A&M came to town in January 1938. Under Coach Ed Gallagher, A&M was a perennial power and defending national champion. A&M would win the title that year and for the next four years after that. Hackney was beginning to make a name for himself on campus, and he was paired that evening with George Chiga, who hailed from Saskatchewan, where he was Canadian National Champion and 1936 Olympian. Chiga won by decision, but Hackney showed that he could fill seats.

On February 25, 1939, a reported crowd of 1,600 turned out to watch the Wildcats pull out a 13.5–12.5 victory over Oklahoma University. The main attraction? Hackney vs. Roland "Waddy" Young. Waddy was an All-American on the powerful Sooner football team and an accomplished wrestler.[13] To add to the pre-match hype, Hackney planned to compete in an indoor track meet at the University of Nebraska the day before and arrive in time for the OU dual the next day:

> 1600 persons, the largest crowd in Kansas State's history, boomed out a thunderous roar when Elmer, who had just returned from Lincoln where he broke

another shot put mark, wandered into Nichols gym shortly after the Wildcat-Oklahoma mat meet had started to complete an iron-man stunt by facing Waddy Young... Sooner Coach Paul Keen objected when Hackney entered the ring in trunks instead of wrestling tights. But he glanced at the "One Man Gang" and accepted Coach B.R. Patterson's explanation that there wasn't a pair of tights in town big enough."[14]

As impressive as his accomplishments on the mat and gridiron were, it was his shot-putting skills that earned him national recognition. Crowds would form when it was his turn to toss the sixteen-pound ball. During his junior season alone, he broke eighteen records.

On May 6, 1939, at a triangular meet in Manhattan against Nebraska and Kansas University, he threw 55' 11" to set the American record, which stood for the next eleven years. A month later, he won his second National Intercollegiate title in Los Angeles with a meet record of 55' 10 3/8".[15] At nationals, a representative from Warner Brothers approached Hackney about the possibility of a career in motion pictures. Nothing ever came of it, but the possibility added to his mystique on the K-State campus.

He was pursuing the world mark going into his senior season when a hand injury from football sidelined him and eventually forced him to throw left-handed. If not for the injury, Coach Haylett was confident he would have eclipsed the 57' 1" record held by Jack Torrance of LSU. "I sincerely believe Hackney had a strong chance to set a new world record. He had excellent speed across the circle and fine coordination as well as a wealth of power," said Haylett.[16]

Hackney was a celebrity at K-State and was named "Most Glamorous" in a campus-wide vote. His story, however, is not without setbacks or tragedy.

There were untimely injuries. His football injuries likely prevented him from All-American status and an early-round NFL draft pick. The hand injury wrecked his chances at a world record in the shot put.

The WWII-related cancellation of the 1940 Olympics removed a stage that may have catapulted him to Weissmuller-status as an actor with his good looks and presence.[17] An Olympic Trials for track and field to determine the Olympic Team in case the games would be back on did not take place. Had there been an Olympics, Hackney was predicted to be on Team USA based on the distance he had thrown and his consistency.

As far as wrestling is concerned, an injury-free Hackney may have been inclined to give it a go his senior year, a move that would likely have garnered him All-American honors.

The athletic setbacks were one thing, but the low point in his life may have occurred on April 8, 1939, with the death of his son. Elmer had just returned from the Texas Relays on April 1st, where he set a meet record of 52' 3 ¼". Elmer and Ellen were expecting their first child in June, but Ellen went into labor two months early and delivered a baby boy, Phillip Joe Hackney, on April 6th. Two days later, he succumbed to complications from the premature birth and died.

The couple had a daughter, Betty, born in 1941 in Pittsburgh while Elmer was playing for the Steelers, and twin daughters, Judy and Trudy, born in 1945 in Manhattan.

In August 1960, fifteen-year-old Judy went missing. Newspaper notices covered the disappearance, and Ellen penned a heartfelt letter to the editor pleading for Judy's safe return. She was gone for months before returning and eventually left again this time for good. The strained relationship between Judy, Trudy, and their parents continued for a lifetime. The twins eventually settled in Mississippi, where they lived for the remainder of their lives.

On October 30, 1968, twenty-seven-year-old Betty, who was married to James Gilmore, was killed in an auto accident in Abilene. Their daughter Jamie (5) and son Robert (4) were in the car with her. The children were taken to Memorial Hospital, where Robert was listed in serious condition. Jamie was transferred to St. John's Hospital in Salina, where she was reported in satisfactory condition with a fractured arm.

On May 30, 1969, fifty-two-year-old Elmer "One Man Gang" Hackney died of a heart attack at home while reading the newspaper in bed.

Only seven months had passed since his daughter's accident, but Betty's death took a toll on him. He struggled daily to cope and make sense of the tragedy until his passing. In Ellen's estimation, the death of their daughter was so hard on her husband that she feels it contributed to his death. "Grandma always thought that he died of a broken heart because it was so hard on him," said granddaughter Jamie Garten while reflecting during an interview in her home in Abilene in 2023.

Jamie remembers spending a lot of time with her grandparents and even living with them for a time after the accident. She reflects fondly on the time she spent with them and has good memories surrounding her grandpa. There was watching football on TV, fishing, and wearing his oversized white T-shirt as a nightgown. Over fifty years later, you can tell by her enthusiasm and genuine smile as she reminisces that her grandpa was special to her, not for scoring touchdowns with defenders hanging off him, or heaving the shot like a rocket, or packing Nichols Hall to the rafters while winning wrestling matches. To her, he was "Grandpa," and she loved spending time with him and tagging along on errands.

Jamie wants the K-State faithful to know that he was a good athlete, a good man, and a hard worker. "Grandpa was proud of K-State and the Manhattan community. He considered that his home," she said.

Manhattan was always home base during the off-season at the time of his participation in the NFL, but after the glory days of his playing career ended, Elmer returned permanently to Kansas to make his home in Manhattan, where he worked for the Mont Green Construction Company as a superintendent.

Ellen eventually met her high school graduation requirements and took classes at K-State. She was active in the Manhattan community, volunteering and hosting social engagements. She lived to be 94 years old and passed away in Abilene in 2010.

With time and perspective, Hackney may be considered the greatest all-around athlete to compete for the Wildcats. He has been enshrined in several halls of fame, including the K-State Athletics Hall of Fame (1991) and the Kansas Sports Hall of Fame (2003). In today's environment of sports specialization and year-round competitions, we may never again see the likes of the One Man Gang.

Elmer and Ellen Hackney. The photo is undated but believed to be around the time of Elmer's death in 1969. *Photo Credit*: Jami Garten collection.

Chapter Three Endnotes: *One Man Gang*

1. "Any person who served at least 90 days in the Union army or navy during the late war is entitled to enter, as a Homestead, one hundred and sixty acres on the alternate reserved sections of public land within railroad limits... Homesteads are free from taxation and cannot be taken away or sold for debt, but are absolutely secure to the settler, as long as he occupies and cultivates the land... offering to every soldier an opportunity to become the owner of a comfortable home, and the possessor of competence and independence." *Maquoketa Excelsior* (Iowa) January 4, 1872.

2. The spelling "Frances Neels" is what appears on the marriage certificate. Her first name was also found to be spelled "Francis" and last name alternatively "Neals" and "Neils."

3. Sod houses were common for settlers in western Kansas. The "soddy" was quick to construct and used ready materials from the surrounding land. They were basic, but kept families protected from the elements and were easy to abandon if the homesteader decided to move on before land ownership was in their name.

4. Gerald, a rigger in the oil fields of west Texas, was tragically killed in 1956 when an oil well exploded. He was only 29 and left a wife, Gladys (youngest sibling of Elmer's wife, Ellen), and four young sons.

5. The state swim meet was also canceled in 1935 for reasons of poor participation numbers. "Due to the scattered interest and inability to make satisfactory provisions for state meets this year, it was voted to discontinue the state championship swimming and wrestling meets temporarily," *The Kansas Athlete*, March – April, 1935.

6. The Missouri Valley A.A.U tournament was in its fifth year in 1935. Coach Patterson developed the event as a way for his athletes to stay active, especially in the era when college freshmen could not compete on the varsity team. It was also presumably a recruiting tool for Patterson, as high school seniors were allowed to participate (and judging from Hackney's participation, underclassmen that were worthy as well). The height of the tournament may have been 1936 when it served as a preliminary Olympic Trials qualifier. Records were found through 1940 when the event was in its eleventh year. K-State won the team title during, at least, the first eleven years in a row.

7. *The Manhattan Mercury,* September 22, 1938.

8. *Lincoln Nebraska State Journal,* November 25, 1938.

9. *The Morning Chronicle,* November 25, 1938.

10. *Lincoln Nebraska Star Journal,* November 25, 1938.

11. The Boston Yanks were a National Football League (NFL) team from 1944-48.

12. *The Herndon Nonpareil* (Nebraska), December 7, 1944.

13. Waddy played in the NFL and later joined the WWII effort, becoming a B-29 Superfortress pilot. Waddy along with his crew were killed in action in January 1945. Read more in "The War Years" chapter.

14. *The Manhattan Mercury,* February 27, 1939. The story of Hackney's thighs being too large for a standard sized wrestling singlet was apparently true. His wife, it is said, had to custom tailor the singlets herself.
15. Hackney won the 1938 NCAAs in Minneapolis with a throw of 51' 81/2".
16. *The Emporia Gazette* (Kansas), January 9, 1940.
17. Johnny Weissmuller was a star swimmer and water polo player in the 1924 and 1928 Olympics for Team USA. He then became one of the most recognized actors of the day, playing Tarzan in a dozen films, among many other film credits. According to Elmer's widow, Ellen, in a 2001 written account, the aforementioned inquiry from Warner Brothers while at the 1939 NCAA Track and Field championships in Los Angeles was in regard to playing a "sub or replacement" role for Weissmuller.

-4-
The War Years

History has shown that December 7, 1941, was indeed a "day that would live in infamy." World War II's social, economic, and cultural impacts are without precedent in U.S. history and within the history of NCAA wrestling.

During the COVID-19 pandemic of 2020, the NCAA halted its national championship competitions in all divisions that were to take place in the spring. Comparisons were made to the situation that college athletics faced after the Japanese bombed Pearl Harbor, bringing the United States fully into the war effort. That comparison is shortsighted and ignorant of the scope and longevity of the sacrifices made during the early to mid-1940s.

The 1942 NCAA championships were held March 27-28 on the campus of Michigan State University. Oklahoma A&M, with its four individual champions, topped the host school by five points for the team title.

Kansas State was represented in East Lansing by Mel Stiefel (121-pound weight class from Gypsum), Leo Wempe (155-pound weight class from Frankfort), and Paul Chronister (175-pound weight class from Chapman). Stiefel and Wempe both went 0-1 in the era when a loss on the front side of the bracket meant your opponent had to reach the finals to stay alive in the consolation bracket. Chronister had a great tournament. He was unseeded but went 4-1 and placed third. His only loss was a 7-4 setback to #1 seed and defending NCAA Champion Dick DiBatista of the University of Pennsylvania. DiBatista would win his second title in '42 and is still considered one of the all-time greats for the Quakers.

The looming WWII moratorium was already being felt at the 1942 NCAA tournament. By comparison, the 1941 event drew one hundred twenty-nine competitors from thirty-eight different schools for an average bracket size of sixteen participants. In 1942 the total was seventy-nine participants for a ten-per-weight class average.[1] Just twenty-three schools were represented in that total.

The A&M Aggies would host and win the next NCAA tournament, but they would have to wait four years to hoist the trophy overhead in Gallagher Hall[2] in March 1946.

Critical decisions were made in the spring of '42 for how the war years would be treated in college athletics. At many institutions, wrestling was put on the shelf, along with other programs categorized as "minor sports." Some decisions were made at the conference level and governed how member schools were made to enforce the restrictions. At the same time, football and basketball were allowed to continue with a more limited schedule in most areas of the country.

An interesting situation evolved when the Army Air Corp's four pre-flight training schools assembled football teams with outstanding players and coaches. The University of North Carolina, the University of Iowa, the University of Georgia, and Saint Mary's University of California hosted these training schools. It was big news when Notre Dame blanked the Iowa Pre-Flight Seahawks 28-0. The Seahawks were coached by the University of Minnesota's Bernie Bierman, who led the Golden Gophers to five national titles between 1934 and '41.

The pre-flight schools and other military teams played for three seasons (1942-44) and were competitive at a time when many college athletic departments were operating at skeletal capacity or not at all, and military teams filled the void. The Seahawks finished second to Notre Dame in the final 1943 Associated Press ranking.

On May 18, 1942, Kansas State announced that the baseball season was canceled per orders from its athletics council. The same announcement revealed that only football, outdoor track and field, and basketball would continue competing during the next school year and would likely be the only sports on campus through the war years.

By late summer, the thought of a 1942-43 wrestling season was not even a discussion. Instead, new military roles for coaches and graduated athletes were made known. Coach Patterson entered the service in July and was reassigned as an instructor in the Department of Military Science and Tactics, leaving him no time to serve as wrestling coach. He was later deployed to England and France with the athletic division, Special Service section of Headquarters with the U.S. Army. He did not return to campus until the summer of 1946.

Pat continued to coach when deployed. He assembled a formidable team of U.S. Army soldiers during his time overseas. The group won the European Theatre of Operations (ETO) championship. When he returned to his post at K-State, a few of his charges from the military enrolled at K-State and joined the wrestling team.

Beyond the loss of college sports seasons, war is real; lives were altered and even lost to the cause. Somber newspaper headlines detailed the horrors and honored those who had been killed or were missing in action from each athletic squad at K-State and throughout the Big Six conference.

In the previous chapter, *One Man Gang*, Walter R. "Waddy" Young of Oklahoma University was mentioned as a competitor of Elmer Hackney. After college, Waddy was selected in the third round of the NFL draft and played two seasons with the Brooklyn Dodgers. In 1941, he voluntarily gave up his NFL career to join the United States Army Air Corps.

He was eventually given the responsibility of piloting a B-29 Superfortress. Beloved by his crew, they named themselves and the craft "Waddy's Wagon." Instead of depicting a scantily-clad woman on the bomber's nose, as was common, a caricature of the crew was painted on Waddy's B-29. After a successful air raid over Tokyo in late 1944, a picture of the crew reenacting the painting with the plane in the background ran in newspapers across the country.

When returning from a mission in January 1945, Waddy became aware of a fellow bomber who was caught in a kamikaze attack. He turned Waddy's Wagon around and flew into enemy fire to protect the plane and return both safely to base. Instead, the planes collided and crashed into the sea.

The photo of Waddy's Wagon, plane, and crew was reprinted in the April 1945 edition of *National Geographic*. The craft is also seen in a government film from 1945, *Target Tokyo*.

After a stellar career on the gridiron and mat at Oklahoma University, Walter "Waddy" Young left the NFL to join the war effort. The beloved pilot and his crew were lost when his plane went down under enemy fire. *Photo Credit*: Department of Defense. Department of the Army. Fort Leavenworth, Kansas. Series: Signal Corps Photograph Collection: Equipment File, 1939 to 1965.

Young accumulated approximately 9,000 combat hours with missions in the Pacific and European Theaters. Waddy and crew were officially declared Killed in Action on January 10, 1946.

The 29-year-old Ponca City native left behind a wife, Maxine (Moody). Young was awarded the Air Medal and Purple Heart. He is memorialized at the Tablets of the Missing at Honolulu Memorial, Honolulu, Hawaii.

All told, an estimated five hundred amateur athletes from the United States lost their lives fighting for freedom in WWII. Among them were several nationally-known college athletes who didn't survive the war.

1939 Heisman Trophy winner Nile Kinnick of the University of Iowa died in June 1943 when his plane went down in the Gulf of Paria off the coast of Venezuela. The 24-year-old Navy pilot enlisted in the Naval Air Reserve after one year of law school at the University of

Iowa, just three days before the attack on Pearl Harbor. Kinnick Hall, a large recreation center on the Olathe Naval Air station in Kansas, was named in his honor.[3]

Nile Kinnick, of the University of Iowa, won the Heisman Trophy in 1939. The Navy aviator lost his life when his plane went down in the Gulf of Paria off the coast of Venezuela in 1943. (picture of Kinnick in flight suit taken at Fairfax Field, north of Kansas City in January 1942). *Photo Credit*: Nile C. Kinnick Papers, Special Collection & Archives, The University of Iowa Libraries.

Al Blozis, former Georgetown University tackle and national indoor and outdoor shot-put champion, was killed in action in the Vosges Mountains in France.

Notre Dame's Jack Chevigny was a star on the gridiron and coached with Knute Rockne after graduating while earning his law degree. He became head coach for the Chicago Cardinals of the NFL and later for the University of Texas.

Chevigny joined the U.S. Marines at thirty-six years old when physical standards were relaxed. He was initially rejected for service with the U.S. Army due to a knee injury from football. He died on February 19, 1945, on the beaches of Iwo Jima.

Marine captain Charlie Paddock, known to many as the world's fastest human while representing the University of Southern California and Team USA, died in a plane crash near Sitka, Alaska.

The K-State wrestling program was not immune from the ultimate sacrifice. First Lieutenant Lowell "Elvis" McCutchen (Kingman), Second Lieutenant Jerald Porter (Norton), Captain Ray Rokey (Sabetha), and Colonel Dean Swift (Olathe) were K-State wrestlers listed among the casualties.

Ray Rokey was a three-sport stand-out for the Wildcats. He was also an outstanding student and involved in campus politics. Rokey lost his life on a battlefield in France in WWII. *Photo Credit*: Collegian Media Group.

McCutchen was a three-sport athlete, lettering in wrestling, football, and track and field for the Cats. He set the school record in the javelin at 187' 9" after taking up the event only during his senior year of college.

McCutchen earned his Bachelor of Science in Physical Education from K-State in May of 1940. He taught and coached at Hiawatha High School when he was called to duty after starting his career at Moline High School. The first lieutenant in the U.S. Army was Killed in Action on December 21, 1944. He was laid to rest in the Walnut Hill Cemetery in Kingman.

Porter, a 1936 state champion for Norton, was on the K-State wrestling team with his older brother Leland, who was NCAA runner-up at 155 pounds in 1941. Jerald was married on December 3, 1942, to Patience Irene Hodgson of Little River and was called to duty in July 1943 along with sixty other K-State R.O.T.C. grads. The U.S. Army Second Lieutenant was killed in action on February 24, 1945, along the Maas River near Roermond, Holland. He was laid to rest in the Netherlands American Cemetery, Margraten, Netherlands.

Rokey, stationed in Germany with the First Army, died of injuries from a battle in France on November 7, 1944. At the time of his death, he was engaged to Martha Hemphill (a Chanute native). He was a three-sport letterman for the Wildcats, participating in wrestling, football, and baseball. The heavyweight wrestler was a running back and quarterback on the football team. He was a pitcher on the baseball team and was named co-captain during his senior season when he had the team's highest batting average.

Rokey was also voted vice president of the K-State Student Council and named Outstanding Student of Kansas State College, Division of Agriculture, for the 1941-42 school year. The distinction was given to only a single student in each of K-State's six departments. Rokey earned a degree in agronomy.

Ray's younger brother Ned followed in his footsteps, succeeding in the classroom and participating in three sports at K-State. However, his time on the wrestling team was short-lived, as he was set to participate in the 1942-43 season, which never happened. Ned also served in WWII.

Swift was a four-year member of the wrestling team, competing in the heavyweight and light-heavyweight divisions. He was also a member of the football team.

He graduated from K-State with a degree in civil engineering and was a prominent student in the department. He was also a lieutenant colonel in K-State's R.O.T.C. regiment.

In the spring of 1935, he was summoned to Washington, D.C., to receive the prestigious Pershing Medal, which General John J. Pershing presented to him personally.

Swift married fellow K-State grad Rita Brown of Edmond, Oklahoma, on June 6, 1936. At the time of his death, the couple was living with their three children in Fort Smith, Arkansas, where he was employed with the Works Projects Administration (WPA).

After serving with the Engineer Corps in Africa, Italy, and Germany, he was sent to the Philippines. He died of complications from polio on January 7, 1946, when stationed in Manila. He was set to return home on a 45-day leave when he took a turn for the worse and passed away.

Swift, an army colonel, was buried in the Manila American Cemetery in Manila, Philippines. He was awarded the Legion of Merit, Bronze Star, and Purple Heart.

Ernest Jessup's story is not widely known, but it should be. He retired as an Army Colonel and received several medals for his service, including the Distinguished Service Cross, the Purple Heart, the Silver Star, the Brown Star, and the Philippine Liberation Medal.

Jessup was born in Cheney on December 29, 1914, and graduated from Wichita East in 1933. He was part of the mighty Blue Aces wrestling program and won a pair of individual state championships in '32 and '33 when his team finished as champion and runner-up.

Jessup was a superstar at K-State. He was part of the celebrated football team known as "Pappy's Boys," which won the Big Six title in 1934 under the leadership of thirty-two year-old Lynn "Pappy" Waldorf. He was also a catcher on the baseball team and was one of the most accomplished Wildcat matmen in program history, winning the Big Six Championship and finishing as NCAA runner-up at 155 pounds in 1937.

In addition to his success on the college mats, qualifying for the 1936 Berlin Olympics was also a goal for Jessup. He entered the first step of the qualifying process in the spring of his junior year. The annual Missouri Valley A.A.U. tournament, held in Nichols Hall in late March, served as one of sixteen district qualifiers across the U.S. He won the welterweight (72 kilograms/158 pounds) bracket by earning a close victory in the finals over 1934 NCAA champion Marion Foreman from the University of Oklahoma.[4]

Jessup next competed in Chicago, where one of three Olympic Trials semifinals occurred at DePaul University. He finished in fourth place with a 4-2 record that included two one-point losses to qualify for the final trials to be held on the campus of Lehigh University in Bethlehem, Pennsylvania, April 16-18, 1936.

Unfortunately, Jessup injured his shoulder and did not get clearance from his doctor in time to compete, preventing him from pursuing his Olympic dream. Ironically, the left shoulder injury did not prevent him from playing baseball. During the final Olympic Trials at Lehigh, he was in Norman, starting as the catcher for the K-State vs. Oklahoma baseball series.

Jessup, whose degree was in industrial journalism,[5] worked as a stereotyper[6] for the *Mercury-Chronicle* during college. After graduation, he accepted a position as a physical education teacher and wrestling coach at Colby High School. However, Uncle Sam came calling for a one-year commitment to active duty from his post in the Army Reserves. That commitment turned into a years-long journey.

K-State grad Ernest Jessup was a standout athlete. He was a catcher on the baseball team, a member of the historic 1934 football team that won the Big Six title, and 1937 Big Six champion and NCAA runner-up at 155 pounds. Jessup went on to serve with distinction in WWII. *Photo Credit*: Collegian Media Group.

In July of 1940, Jessup was assigned as an instructor in the military science and tactics department at K-State. He served in that position for two years. Ironically, Jessup's replacement was his college wrestling coach, Buel Patterson, who was recently ordered to active duty. "I am proud to have the opportunity of joining the U.S. armed forces, and I'm happy to remain here at K-State where most of my friends are," said Patterson at the time.[7]

Jessup requested to leave his post at K-State to join his father-in-law, Major General Frank C. Mahin, who had recently taken over as commanding officer of the 33rd Infantry Division at Camp Forrest, Tennessee. Jessup's position was serving as an aide to the major general.

As fate would have it, after less than two months in Tennessee, Jessup's father-in-law was killed in the crash of an army observation plane near Waynesboro, Tennessee. Mahin, along with two army fliers: Second Lieutenant Robert Turk, the pilot, and Sergeant John Camerford, were killed when the plane struck a tree. The trio was en route to Fort Sill, Oklahoma.

A year after graduating from Harvard in 1909, the fifty-four-year-old major general joined the Army. His thirty-two-year career in the regular army included service in WWI. Among his training and education experiences was graduating from the general staff school at Ft. Leavenworth in Kansas.

The news of the crash shocked the military sector and ran in newspapers across the U.S. and on radio news bulletins from coast to coast. Mahin left a wife and four children, including a son, Frank, Jr., a cadet at West Point. He was given full military honors and was buried in Arlington National Cemetery.

From Camp Forrest in Tennessee, Jessup served for two years in New Guinea, Morotai, and Luzon in the Philippines, one of the war's most volatile regions.

The following account of a firefight that landed him in Walter Reed for months of rehab is chilling. It is from the War Department's Bureau of Public Relations press release that appeared in the July 19, 1945 edition of the *Manhattan Republic*.

> Severely wounded but ordering his men to take cover and make no attempt to rescue him, Lieutenant Colonel Ernest D. Jessup, Infantry battalion

commander, remained in an exposed jungle clearing to direct the brilliant flanking attack and capture of a strong Japanese salient on Luzon. Colonel Jessup's hard-hitting battalion had been in combat continuously for more than two months when he fell on April 21, permanently disabled by Japanese machine gun and mortar fire. The entire fighting was over extremely rough terrain and against fierce enemy resistance.

The Japanese were well-dug-in, well-equipped, and fanatical in their determination to hold these dominating positions at all costs. In all engagements, Colonel Jessup had constantly directed operations from the front lines.

The enemy, well entrenched in holes and caves on the steep slopes, waited until two platoons of Doughboys began to cross a small clearing on the ridge before opening fire with machine guns. The fire pinned down both platoons and effectively blocked further advance.

Colonel Jessup detected the enemy gun positions but could not adjust mortar or artillery fire without endangering his own men. Instead, he gave a third platoon the mission of knocking out the Japanese gun. It was necessary to mark the well-hidden target for the platoon leader, however, and another officer with Colonel Jessup emptied his carbine into the enemy strongpoint.

This action, however, served to disclose the battalion commander's location to the Japanese and while Colonel Jessup was observing the progress of the assault platoon and also trying to obtain tank support by radio, he was hit by a burst of machine gun fire.

Although seriously wounded in the chest, right leg and left arm by machine gun bullets and hit again, almost immediately, by fragments of Japanese mortar shell, he continued to direct the operation and forbade his men to attempt his rescue.

Under Colonel Jessup's continued direction—he was scarcely able to talk because of his chest wound—the Japanese strongpoint was successfully flanked and three machine guns, four knee mortars, and quantities of ammunition were captured. Eight Japanese were killed at their guns and 15 others who fled into the valley below were killed by other members of the 33rd or "Illinois" Division.

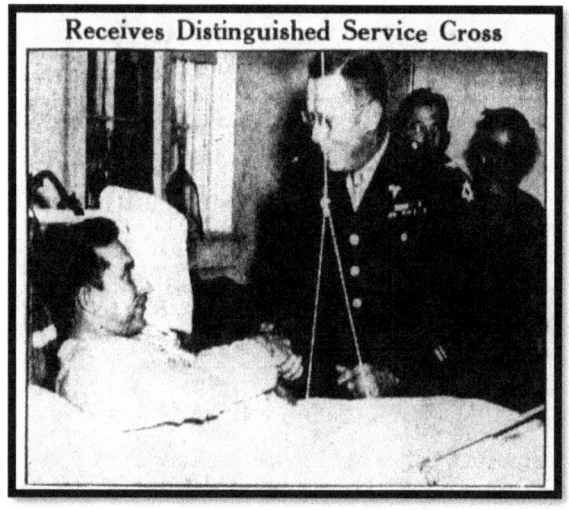

Receives Distinguished Service Cross

While serving in the Philippines during WWII, Ernest Jessup was injured in a battle where he sacrificed his own life for his troops and advanced his company's position against the Japanese. *Photo Credit: Manhattan Mercury.*

That gripping account demonstrates the horrors of war and how Jessup found a way to survive in the face of impossible odds. At the time, he had a wife and three young children at home in Manhattan.

Prior to his time in Walter Reed National Military Medical Center in Bethesda, Maryland, Jessup was first admitted to a local hospital in the Pacific to treat his life-threatening injuries and to stabilize him for the long journey home.

Jessup spent months in Walter Reed and Winter General Hospital in Topeka. Part of his time in Winter General coincided with Bob

Dole's recovery from injuries sustained in fighting in Italy. Dole, of Russell, Kansas, went on to serve in the U.S. Senate from 1969 to 1996 and was the Republican Party's nominee for president in 1996 when Bill Clinton defeated him.

Jessup faced a lifetime of rehab and physical limitations from his injuries; nevertheless, he went on to lead a productive life. He died May 12, 1988, one month after he and his wife Anna (Mahin) celebrated their 50th wedding anniversary. He was laid to rest in the Fort Riley Post Cemetery near Junction City, Kansas. Ernest and Anna raised five children.

Even though competition had resumed in the Big Six and nationwide for most schools during the 1945-46 season, Coach Patterson was still deployed, so the university decided to wait until his return before resuming competition at the varsity level. In his absence, Fritz Knorr, who served as head basketball coach from 1944 to 1946, was assigned the job of active wrestling coach to make sure minimum responsibilities were given attention. Knorr was also an assistant coach for the football team and later head coach of the baseball team. This is, of course, the same Fritz Knorr who would take over as head wrestling coach in 1953.

Coach Buel Patterson served in the U.S. Army during WWII. He returned in 1946 from a deployment in the European Theatre. He was also part of the ROTC program while an undergrad at Oklahoma A&M.
Photo Credit: Maureen Berkemeyer collection.

When Patterson returned for the 1946-47 season, enthusiasm was plenty, and hopes were high for a good bounce-back season. A group of seventy-five turned out for tryouts. When the dust cleared, thirty-five men from six different states populated the first post-war roster for one of the largest and most diverse teams in the program's history. Not surprisingly, the team members were almost all new to the program. Only Warren Boring (Kansas City), Verle McClellan (Wichita), and Bob Johnson (Hutchinson) had previous experience on the Wildcat squad. Boring and McClellan were last on the team during the 1940-41 season, a six-year hiatus! Only Johnson returned from the last pre-war roster, 1941-42. Almost 80 percent of the 1946-47 roster did not return the following season.

It was also Pat's last season in Manhattan after twenty years at the helm. He would go on to successful stints at the University of Nebraska and the University of Illinois before retiring in 1968 after forty-one years as a college head coach at three major NCAA institutions.

Like the COVID-restriction years, the WWII moratorium was handled differently within individual programs and conferences. A case in point is K-State. Its decision to wait a year after the restrictions were lifted likely set the program back. One has to wonder if it was also a factor in Patterson's exit to Nebraska.

It wasn't only K-State that was slow to emerge from the WWII shutdown. Only seventeen teams were represented at the first post-WWII NCAA tournament in 1946, the lowest representation of schools in the event's history, which dates back to 1928.

1936 NCAA Champion Oklahoma University was in worse shape than K-State in its return to the mat. A September 1946 letter to the editor in the OU student newspaper, *The Oklahoma Daily*, questioned the school's commitment to its wrestling program. "The university, as far as sports are concerned, is a wrestling school in a wrestling state. The reason for discontinuation was 'the disinclination of other Big Six schools' to reinstate this sport. Yet, Oklahoma has re-activated other sports which will see no Big Six competition." Bob Payne's letter went on to state, "...the university's main source of competition in wrestling, the state of Oklahoma itself, continued through the war to be the beehive of wrestling interest. Most of its schools always strong in the sport never dropped it at all. Others reactivated it at the earliest opportunity." In OU's case, a patchwork of coaches (including no coach at all) during the war years preceded the hiring of 1935 NCAA All-American Port Robinson.[8] He was not hired until mid-December 1946, coinciding with the announcement that the program would be reinstated at the start of the second semester.

The WWII era in college sports was a rough patch, and getting back to business as usual took time. For Kansas State wrestling, the shutdown happened twenty years after the program was established and was a critical time for a coaching change. At the time, nobody would have guessed that a permanent shutdown would be looming three decades over the horizon.

Chapter Four Endnotes: *The War Years*

1. From 1928 until 1951 there were eight weight contests at the NCAAs, with the exception of 1928, 1932, and 1936 when there were seven. From 1952 to present, ten weight classes have been contested, with the exception of 1966 through 1969 when there were eleven.
2. Gallagher Hall, built in 1939, was renamed Gallagher-Iba Arena in 1987 when it was remodeled.
3. The building no longer exists, and the site is now the New Century AirCenter.
4. Foreman won his NCAA title in the 165-pound weight class.
5. The industrial journalism degree required students to take courses in home economics, agriculture, and engineering, in addition to reporting and copy editing. The degree evolved and expanded over time and eventually became known as mass communications.
6. A newspaper stereotyper's job was to create lead plates imprinted with the day's news for the printing press to print its run. The work was exacting, fast-paced, and physically demanding.
7. *Manhattan Republic*, May 5, 1942.
8. Robinson finished in third place at 165 pounds.

-5-
From Wrestling to Rasslin'

Joe Blanchard was born December 7, 1928, in Haskell, Oklahoma. The family relocated to southeast Kansas, where they settled in Cherryvale. Blanchard grew up doing farm work and playing baseball and football.

He enrolled in Cherryvale High School and spent his first three years there. Due to his father's employment, the family moved to nearby Parsons in October of Joe's senior year. The standout football player for Cherryvale opened the 1945 season with a 19-0 loss to the school he would be playing for only weeks later!

As a junior at Cherryvale High School in 1945, Blanchard played on the basketball team. He was not introduced to the sport of wrestling until he enrolled at K-State.
Photo Credit: Cherryvale Historical Museum.

After graduating from Parsons High in May 1946, he attended Kansas State University, where he accepted a scholarship to play football.

By the end of October 1946, Coach Hobbs Adams moved Blanchard from the "B" team to varsity at left tackle. He became a standout player by his senior year with all-conference accolades. He was also named co-captain of the team. It is unclear, however, when he decided to add wrestling to his plate or even when he took the sport up for the first time.

Wrestling was not offered at Parsons High until the early 1970s and was unavailable in Cherryvale during Blanchard's formative years. It was not uncommon for football linemen to fill in at heavyweight on college wrestling rosters during the era, so it can only be assumed that Coach Patterson saw the potential in Blanchard and recruited him after he was already on campus.

Coach Pat left for the University of Nebraska after Blanchard's freshman year. He continued to compete under the guidance of Coach Leon "Red" Reynard for the rest of his college career, and he developed into a formidable opponent.

Blanchard's biggest achievement was the Big Seven title he captured in 1950. He had a tournament to remember. The team, however, finished only fourth out of five teams, behind Oklahoma, Nebraska, and Iowa State, ahead of only Colorado.

In the finals, Blanchard met "Iron" Mike DiBiase. DiBiase was also a lineman on the Cornhusker football team and quickly made a name for himself after his college days were over on the professional wrestling circuit. His adopted son, Ted, would go on to international stardom as The Million Dollar Man in the WWE.[1]

Epic battle with Nebraska's Mike DiBiase. Blanchard won the Big Seven title over the three-time defending champion. *Photo Credit*: Collegiate Media Group.

Going into the finals of the 1950 Big Seven tournament, all of the elements of a Cinderella story were in place. DiBiase was the three-time defending Big Seven champion[2] and the 1946 AAU national champion. The year prior, DiBiase and the Cornhuskers won their first-ever Big Seven wrestling title under the direction of Coach Patterson, the same former K-State coach who was likely responsible for introducing Blanchard to the sport of wrestling. To top it off, the event took place in Nichols Hall on the K-State campus.

Blanchard had defeated DiBiase in a dual meet earlier in the season but had not previously placed in the conference tournament.

Ultimately, Blanchard won by the slimmest of margins, claiming the title by referee's decision to cap his career at K-State with one of the most significant victories in the program's history.

The 1950 NCAA tournament was held in the historic West Gym on the campus of Iowa State Teacher's College in Cedar Falls. Blanchard competed there but bowed out with a 0-1 record after the opponent that beat him in the quarterfinals failed to advance to the finals.

1950 Big 7 individual champions. Back row (l-r): Bill Borders (121 lbs., Oklahoma), Joe Butler (165 lbs., Oklahoma), Harold Gilliland (128 lbs., Nebraska), Front row (l-r): Bob Wilson (136 lbs., Iowa State), Herb Reese (175 lbs., Nebraska), Joe Blanchard (Heavyweight, Kansas State), Leonard Marcotte (155 lbs., Oklahoma), George Jackson (145 lbs., Oklahoma).
Photo Credit: Collegiate Media Group.

Blanchard's commitment and steady improvement are testaments to his determination. As a freshman, he was part of the first post-WWII team after the program was put on ice for four seasons. Blanchard, William Brown (who hailed from Larned), and Archie Vernon of Oberlin were the only members who were part of the team each year from 1946-50.

After graduating, Blanchard stayed on to coach the freshman football team for a season before embarking on a professional football career.

Rather than going a more traditional route and playing for a National Football League (NFL) team, he signed on with the Canadian Football League (CFL), where he played from 1951-54. Blanchard was part of the Edmonton Eskimos organization for three seasons and the Calgary Stampeders for his final season in 1954.

JOE BLANCHARD
Plays Tackle
Age: 22; born Haskell, Okla.,
December 7, 1928
Height: 6'1½"; Weight 220
Team last with: Kansas State
College, 1949. Is single.

Blanchard played three seasons with the Edmonton Eskimos of the Canadian Football League (CFL) before spending his final season with the Calgary Stampeders. This is from an Edmonton program during his rookie season.
Photo Credit: Edmonton Elks.

Although his team lost to the Toronto Argonauts, 21-11, he was part of the 1952 Eskimos team that played in the Grey Cup, the Super Bowl of Canadian football.

During the 1953 season, his coach was first-year head coach Darrell Royal. The Hall of Famer started his career in Edmonton before moving on to Mississippi State, the University of Washington, and the University of Texas. He guided the Longhorns to three national titles. The stadium that UT plays in, Darrell K. Royal-Texas Memorial Stadium, is named in his honor.

1953 Edmonton Eskimos team. Blanchard is #60 in the third row. This was his final year playing in the Canadian Football League. Darrell Royal (standing, far left) was the head coach. He went on to a hall of fame career at the University of Texas.
Photo Credit: Edmonton Elks.

Prior to his final football season in Calgary, Blanchard became interested in professional wrestling and began to transition from the gridiron to the ring. He made a connection with the Big Time Wrestling promotion; founded earlier as Stampede Wrestling under the direction of Stu Hart. From there his career took off and he never looked back.

He found success individually and with his tag team partner, Lord James Blears. He held the 50th State Big Time Wrestling Tag Team belt and the NWA Big Time Wrestling Texas Heavyweight Championship belt during his career. His wrestling travels took him to Canada, Japan, Australia, and Hawaii, as well as across the continental United States.

He founded Southwest Championship Wrestling (SCW) in 1978 when he retired from the ring. Blanchard continued to be actively involved in promoting and managing late into life.

His son, Tully, was also a successful professional wrestler after an NCAA D1 college football career at SMU and West Texas State University. He starred in the World Wrestling Federation (WWF) as a member of the Four Horsemen, which consisted of Ric Flair, Arn Anderson, Ole Anderson, and Blanchard. Tully's daughter is Tessa, who made a name for herself in Impact Wrestling. As of this publication, she is still active in the industry as a third-generation professional wrestler.

Blanchard's son Taylor was killed in a car accident in April 1978 when he was just sixteen years old. The death had a profound impact on Joe.

While struggling to overcome the tragedy, he "turned his life over to Jesus Christ." From then on, he was known to give his testimony and evangelize freely. He served at Cornerstone Church in San Antonio for many years until a cancer diagnosis made it too taxing late in life.

Tully recalls his own conversion to Christianity through the persistent prayer of his parents. "My dad came to know the Lord after my brother was killed. Most people don't make a move like that without something monumentous in their life. My brother was killed in 1978 in April, and it changed everything about our family." He went on to say, "It affected me, but it didn't affect me in a spiritual way until 1989; twelve years later. My dad and my mother, when they came to know the Lord, as their personal savior, they prayed for me for twelve years. At the end of twelve years, On November 13, 1989, I said 'Jesus, take over my life.' It's now thirty-some years after that."

Blanchard died on March 22, 2012, in San Antonio, at the age of 83. He was survived by his wife Jackie of fifty-nine years, and son Tully.

He was inducted into the George Tragos/Lou Thesz Professional Wrestling Hall of Fame in 2016. The Hall of Fame is part of the National Wrestling Hall of Fame Dan Gable Museum in Waterloo, Iowa, which was created by Iowa author and historian Mike Chapman and his wife Bev.

Chapter Five Endnotes: *From Wrestling to Rasslin'*

1. Professional wrestling's World Wrestling Entertainment, Inc. company commonly known as WWE.
2. During a brief period when intercollegiate athletics returned after WWII, the NCAA allowed freshmen to participate on the varsity level to encourage participation and help build teams back to pre-war levels. Prior to and after that reprieve, freshmen were not allowed to compete in varsity competitions.

-6-
LegaSeay

College sports programs take pride in producing athletes who make their way in the world and give back. Among that group are those who go on to coach. Kansas State's wrestling program has produced dozens of coaches who have impacted the Kansas and national wrestling landscape.

The K-State coaching legacy is so deep that the following pages highlight only the most accomplished among them. Included are coaches of state champion teams at the high school level in Kansas and those who went on to lead NCAA DI programs.

The list is chronologically ordered by graduation year, except for the first entry, Joe Seay. As the most recognized and accomplished among them, Seay (pronounced "SEE") garners the chapter title and the most attention in the chapter.

Joe Seay – Class of 1963

While head coach at Cal State-Bakersfield, Joe Seay led the Roadrunners to seven NCAA DII titles from 1973-84. *Photo Credit*: California State University, Bakersfield Department of Intercollegiate Athletics.

The highest-profile name among the K-State wrestlers who have achieved the most in the coaching ranks is 1963 grad Joe Seay, who would coach at Oklahoma State and lead the program to back-to-back NCAA titles in 1989 and 1990. He followed that up by leading the 1993 and 1995 USA Wrestling Freestyle teams to the first World Championship titles in history.

Seay was born and raised in Altus, Oklahoma, but moved to south central Kansas at the end of his freshman year of high school, where he graduated from Wellington High School in 1958.

He won the 141-pound state championship as a senior during the single-class era in Kansas, finishing the season undefeated. Coach Ken Spicher, who also wrestled at K-State and was a 1955 grad, encouraged him to pick up the sport when he saw the wiry sixteen-year-old walking the school's hallways only two years before winning state.

Seay went on to a successful college career at K-State. He qualified for the NCAA tournament in 1961, 1962, and 1963, during the era when freshmen could not compete at the varsity level.

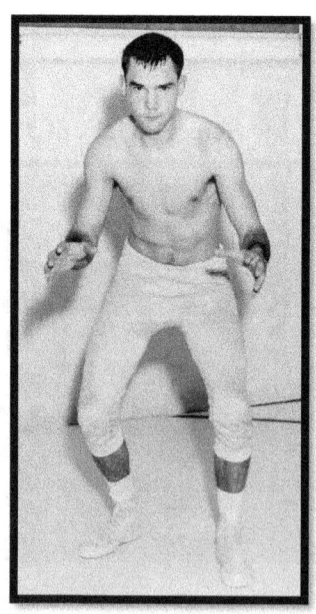

Seay as a senior at K-State in 1963. Photo Credit: Collegiate Media Group.

It is important to note that during Seay's national tournament appearances, a loss on the championship side of the bracket meant that the opponent you lost to had to reach the finals for you to wrestle for All-American status in the consolation bracket.[1] Seay competed at 147 pounds during his entire college career. He went 2-1 at both the 1961 and 1962 NCAA tournaments, losing to eventual All-Americans both years.

In 1963, he went 2-2. He won his first two matches[2] before falling 3-1 in the quarterfinals to the #1 seed and defending NCAA champion, Mike Natvig of Army West Point. Natvig would win his second title and cement himself as the most credentialed Army West Point wrestler ever. As of 2024, he remains the only Black Knight to have ever won an individual NCAA title in the sport of wrestling.

In the "blood round" of the consolation bracket,[3] Seay lost 3-2 in overtime to Dick Slutzky of Syracuse, who eventually placed fourth in the 147-pound bracket.

In wrestling, a loss like that can stick with its owner for decades. To be denied All-American honors (or a national title, for those who reach the finals and finish as runner-up) can gnaw on those who fall short and be taken to unhealthy levels as it spills into their daily life. For others, it can be the inspiration that keeps them going in the sport as a competitor or coach. Seay's loss may have motivated him to keep competing as a post-grad. As a result, countless athletes have benefited from the impact he made through his coaching.

Seay earned his B.A. in physical education in 1963 and an M.S. in P.E. and school administration in 1964 (both from K-State). He also took the LSAT and scored well, but his passion was pursuing his wrestling and coaching goals.

After college, Seay competed in the international styles of freestyle and Greco-Roman wrestling[4] and became a known entity on the circuit. He participated in the 1964, 1968, and 1972 Olympic Trials and had several significant wins along the way.

From Manhattan, he spent time in Wellington preparing for the 1964 Olympic Trials, which were held in New York City. During that time, he trained with 1960 Olympic Champion, Doug Blubaugh, who farmed near Ponca City, Oklahoma, an hour's drive south of Wellington. Richard DeMoss, who was in the area and still training, also attended the practice sessions in Ponca City.

Blubaugh had a key to the school and would let Seay and DeMoss in for daily late-night practice sessions leading up to the trials. Seay credited Blubaugh with much of his technical development and the reason for making the finals at the trails. "We really just did a lot of live wrestling and picked his brain about certain situations and what options we had in those situations. He gave us pointers and we listened to his advice. He was super tough and an Olympic Champion. We got a lot out of those informal practice sessions," said DeMoss as he reflected in 2024.

After the Olympic Trials, Seay and his family left for California, and he began coaching at South High School in Bakersfield in the fall of 1964. He spent eight years there, compiling a dual record of 177-12-2 and earning National Coach of the Year recognition.

In April 1970, Seay entered the national AAU tournament in Lincoln, Nebraska, where he was runner-up to Dan Gable in freestyle.

This was only three weeks after Gable's epic loss to the University of Washington's Larry Owings at the NCAA tournament held on the campus of Northwestern University. Dating back to high school, Gable had been victorious in one hundred eighty-one consecutive matches and would win the 1971 World Championship and the 1972 Munich Olympic Gold before becoming one of the most accomplished college coaches ever, regardless of sport. He led the Iowa Hawkeyes to fifteen NCAA titles, twenty-one Big Ten Championships, and a dual meet record of 355–21–5 in twenty-one seasons with the Hawks.

Seay was also a formidable Greco-Roman wrestler. In May of 1970, he won the USWF Greco-Roman nationals at 68 kilograms (149.5 pounds) in Fullerton, California. All told, Seay won three national Greco-Roman titles while placing second twice in freestyle.

At the final 1972 Olympic Trials competition, held at Anoka, Minnesota, Seay again lost to Gable in the finals. In that competition, much was made of Owings entering and losing to Gable by a 7-1 score.

The single point scored by Owings would be the only point Gable surrendered during the Olympic Trials process through the Munich Games themselves.

Seay's 9-4 victory over Owings in Anoka was less publicized but also notable. That upset may have grabbed the headline absent the Gable storyline.

Gable remembers being unaware of Seay until he began competing against him on the senior level. "He was several years older. Bob Buzzard helped prepare me for Joe and let me know he was a worthy opponent," he said.

"We became friendly as competitors and during our early coaching careers when he was at Bakersfield. It wasn't until he took over at OSU that we became less friendly. As athletes, we were fine. As coaches, we were fine when he was at Bakersfield. When he was at OSU, we were no longer fine. He was brought in to beat Iowa. That's when it was no longer a friendly relationship. He was a determined competitor and wanted to win. I appreciated that about him. He was good for wrestling," Gable explained.

After the 1971-72 season, Seay jumped to coaching at the college level when he moved across town and became the first wrestling coach in the history of California State University, Bakersfield (Cal State-Bakersfield).

He spent the next dozen years at Cal State-Bakersfield building that program into a national power on the NCAA DII *and* DI levels.

For a time in the 1960s through 1992,[5] wrestlers from NCAA DII, and later DIII, programs could qualify for the NCAA DI nationals. In later years qualifying was based on finishing as a finalist (DII) or champion (DIII). Each division also had a wildcard selection process. For a time, the NCAA also allowed top individuals from the NAIA ranks to compete at the NCAA DI and DII nationals.

The CSB Roadrunners won seven NCAA DII titles under Seay's leadership. That tally included a string of four in a row from 1980-83. Incredibly, after the initial three years of building the program from scratch, Seay's teams finished as NCAA DII champion or runner-up every year from 1975-76 through his final season, 1983-84.

The string of consecutive champion and runner-up team finishes is impressive. However, the string of eight years in a row of having at least one NCAA Division I All-American is more impressive.

To put this into perspective, only eight schools had at least one DI All-American each year from 1977-84, and only four of those schools had more NCAA champions than Cal State-Bakersfield. Those schools? The University of Iowa (59 All-Americans, 15 NCAA champions), Iowa State University (48 AAs, 8 champions), Oklahoma State University (42 AAs, 11 champions), Oklahoma University (34 AAs, 8 champions), the University of Wisconsin (24 AAs, 5 champions), Lehigh University (24 AAs, 4 champions), Arizona State University (19 AAs, 0 champions), and Cal State-Bakersfield (16 AAs, 6 champions).

Of the Roadrunner All-Americans, an incredible 37 percent were national champions. Those champions came in five consecutive years from 1980-84; Joe Gonzales and John Azevedo (1980), Dan Cuestas (1981 and 1982), Adam Cuestas (1983), and Jesse Reyes (1984).

In a 2024 interview from his home in California, Azevedo spoke of the improbability of a school like Cal State-Bakersfield working its way into the national conversation of top teams. "We had a small budget. Our room was only a little more than the size of a full mat. Scholarships were not fully funded. We had to practice in shifts," he said. He also emphasized Seay's ability to surround himself with good people and not concern himself with being ego-driven and rejecting input from others. If something worked for an athlete, Coach Seay was willing to support it. Azevedo cited examples of highly regarded coaches such as Larry Morgan, Jim Humphrey, and Bruce Burnett contributing to the success of the Bakersfield program.

Burnett, who went on to a hall-of-fame career leading Team USA and the U.S. Naval Academy teams, describes Seay as a, "Gentle spirit that could fight at the drop of a hat. He was a nice guy and a fierce competitor." Burnett added, "Joe was not the most organized big picture guy, but was gifted in understanding strengths and weaknesses of his athletes and was not intimidated about utilizing those around him to get the most out of his wrestlers."

An impressive 63 percent of the Cal State-Bakersfield All-Americans were NCAA finalists, and 88 percent placed in the top three. Of the sixteen DI All-Americans for CSB during their DII era, the two lowest-place winners were one fourth place and one seventh-place finish.

With eye-popping stats like that, it was no wonder that some DI schools were pushing for a national tournament that did not allow competitors from DII schools to compete.

It should be noted that DII and DIII schools were not allowed to factor into the team scoring. The individual accolades are part of the history books, but the non-DI schools did not appear in the team standings.

Jim Miller was an NCAA DII champion for the University of Northern Iowa in 1974 and 1975. He was also an NCAA DI runner-up in 1974 and a fourth-place finisher in 1975. Miller went on to build a powerhouse NCAA DIII program at Wartburg College in Waverly, Iowa, where he led the Knights to ten national championships.

When asked about his perspective, his measured response is worth noting, given his unique background and credentials. "I miss seeing Division II and Division III people getting the opportunity to go there [to the NCAA DI championships]. I get why Division I doesn't want the other divisions. They have their own qualifier. I get both sides, but I do miss watching that at the Division I tournament. As a Division III coach at Wartburg, I think there were some guys there that could have broken through and got on the podium [in DI]," said Miller.

Joe Gonzales and John Azevedo were Seay's first NCAA DI champions when they won back-to-back titles at 118 pounds and 126 pounds at the 1980 NCAA Championships in Corvallis, Oregon. Both went on to international success on the freestyle circuit.

Azevedo earned a spot on the 1980 U.S. Olympic team that was boycotted and he also finished in fourth place at the 1982 World Championships. He remembers Seay participating in practice as well as putting the team through the paces. "Most of the practices were drilling hard and wrestling hard. Joe and the other coaches would occasionally show technique, but it was mostly learning from each other, and Joe would get in there and scrap like the rest of us," said Azevedo.

After the 1983-84 season, the winds of change were coming, and Seay would be called up to the big leagues.

In the earliest years of college wrestling, Ed Gallagher created unsustainable expectations at Oklahoma State that have continued through the decades. In 1984, those expectations came to a head when the Cowboys finished behind the mighty Hawkeyes of Iowa in the NCAA tournament by a 123.75 – 98 margin.

After a 19-0 dual season that included a 24-6 victory over Iowa, and an NCAA tournament runner-up finish, Athletic Director Myron Roderick had enough of falling short. Long-time coach Tommy Chesbro was fired after fifteen years. Thirteen of Chesbro's teams finished in the top five at nationals, with his 1971 team bringing home the top prize. Expectations were high indeed!

Roderick knew more than a little about winning and wanted the Pokes to be back on top. He was a three-time NCAA champion for OSU and a 1956 Olympian, and he led the program to seven NCAA championships in just thirteen years as head coach.

His target to replace Chesbro was an unconventional idea—none other than Dan Gable, who led Iowa to its seventh straight NCAA title in 1984. According to a Mike Chapman-authored *Cedar Rapids Gazette* article dated March 22, 1984, Gable had been offered a ten-year contract worth $2.5 million. That figure was unheard of in that era.

Roderick denied the claim in an *Oklahoman* article the next day but said that he had been in casual talks with Gable on the topic in recent years and was told by Gable at the 1984 NCAA tournament that he was not interested. In the article, Roderick stated that an actual figure was not discussed.

Some forty years later, Gable remembers the offer and recalls being tempted by the potential of tripling his current salary. After the success that he brought to Iowa, he had not seen a bonus or performance-based raise, so he was impressed with Roderick's proposal.

However, It was a family decision, and Gable's wife, Kathy, creatively let her thoughts be known. Coach Gable recalls his wife asking him if he was planning to come home on weekends if he took the OSU job. "At that point, I knew the deal was off," he said. Kathy is also a native Iowan from the Cedar Valley and liked having family close in familiar surroundings.

Roderick had arranged for a private plane to transport Gable to Stillwater to seal the deal, however, the night before, Gable canceled the trip. Family and familiarity won the day, and Gable remained firmly planted in Iowa City for the remainder of his career and to this day.

At the time, Chesbro was still the coach. Roderick is quoted in *The Oklahoman* article as saying, "I haven't talked with Tommy. I'm going to sit down and talk with him in the morning because I want him to know where I'm coming from too."

Four days after this meeting, on Wednesday, March 28, 1984, Roderick announced that Seay would replace Chesbro. "This is the most difficult decision I've ever made," he said at a news conference.

Seay hoists the NCAA championship trophy overhead in 1989 when the tournament was hosted in Oklahoma City. *Photo Credit*: Oklahoma State University Archives.

Seay was at OSU from 1984-91. The NCAA titles in '89 and '90 were the pinnacle of his career, but the darkest time in program history was an NCAA investigation for relatively minor infractions that led to his firing.

The inquiry took on a life of its own after athletes involved conspired to cover up details and lie to investigators. In the aftermath, Seay was dismissed, and the program was severely penalized. OSU was banned from the 1993 NCAA tournament and recruiting and scholarship restrictions were imposed as well.

The actions were felt individually and in the team race at the NCAAs. Chuck Barbee lost his senior season and was denied a shot at the NCAA crown. Alan Fried would likely have accumulated more accolades than he garnered in his career as a Cowboy. Tony Purler transferred to Nebraska at semester and was NCAA champion two months later. T.J. Jaworsky left for the University of North Carolina and won three NCAA titles and was named the first Dan Hodge Trophy winner after title #3 in 1995. Ray Brinzer went to Iowa and finished in third place at the 1993 NCAAs.

As luck would have it, Pat Smith had a redshirt year to use in 1992-93. Otherwise, his unprecedented fourth NCAA DI title would have happened for another school, or not at all.

Purler's reflection of his former coach includes his dedication and commitment to his athletes and the sport itself. "What I remember most is that he cared about the athletes, and he cared about the sport. He was the type of guy that would give you the shirt off his back," he said.

With limitations on recruiting and scholarships and a less-than-stable coaching situation initially, the rebuilding was not easy. Still, John Smith proved to be the right hire to patch things up and carry on the tradition. OSU was back on top in short order. The Pokes won the 1994 NCAA title by 18.25 points over runner-up Iowa.

Seay also landed back on his feet. He led the USA to its first-ever world titles in freestyle wrestling in 1993 and 1995. He was also the head coach for the 1996 Atlanta Olympics, where the United States captured five medals, including golds from Kendall Cross (57 KG),

Tom Brands (62 KG), and Kurt Angle (100 KG).

Bruce Barnett was on Seay's staff at OSU and also served as National Team coach for many years, helping usher in a new era of success for Team USA in the late 1990s through the first decade of the 2000s.

Coach Seay returned to college coaching for a short time. He was an assistant at the University of Virginia from 2003-05 on coach Lenny Bernstein's staff and head coach during the 2005-06 season at the University of Tennessee at Chattanooga, where he succeeded Terry Brands.

Seay passed away on July 11, 2019. He was 80 years old. In an interview shown in his memorial video, he says, "I think God put me on this earth to be a wrestling coach. I really believe that. My faith in Him gave me the faith in all of the things that I needed to do after that."

Fritz Knorr – Class of 1931

Fritz Knorr, in 1952 while serving as business manager for the athletic department.
He took over as head wrestling coach in 1953.
Photo Credit: Collegiate Media Group.

With the departure of head coach Red Reynard, Fritz Knorr was tapped to lead the program. From 1953 until his death in 1972, Knorr was head coach.

The multi-sport high school athlete from Savannah, Missouri, had limited exposure to the sport of wrestling before enrolling at K-State.

He picked it up after stepping foot on campus and found himself in the lineup on a regular basis.

After college, Knorr taught and coached at the junior high, high school, and junior college levels in Kansas and Missouri. After a decade, he returned to Manhattan, where he was affiliated with K-State until his death.

During his time at K-State, the Wildcats earned five All-American honors (Ken Ellis, Ted Weaver, Don Darter, Bill Brown, and Jerry Cheynet). Ted Weaver and Pat Doyle won individual Big Seven titles during Knorr's era, and John Dooley and John Thompson were Big Eight champions.

Knorr served on the NCAA wrestling rules committee and worked to develop wrestling at the grassroots level in Kansas, where he was involved in coaching education and the promotion of youth wrestling, which is his lasting legacy.

The Kansas Wrestling Coaches Association's (KWCA) annual fall clinic, the "KWCA Fritz Knorr Fall Clinic," bears his name. Knorr began hosting the fall clinic in 1956, picking up on the concept started by Coach Pat Paterson, who started a similar clinic in 1939 that ran through 1946.

In late fall 1972, after Knorr's passing, a group of coaches came together to carry on the clinic and decided to name it in his honor. It has been held annually since 1956. Dr. Harold Nichols, Myron Roderick, Ken Kraft, Dan Gable, Rob Koll, Kevin Jackson, Terry Brands, and Terry Steiner are just a sampling of the clinic's headliners over the years.

In 1964, Knorr was instrumental in starting what is now the USAWKS Kids Folkstyle State Tournament. That first state-wide event was held March 5-6 at Manhattan High School with one hundred twenty-seven entries. 2024 marked the sixty-first annual tournament. The three-day event was contested on eighteen mats and played host to 2,446 athletes representing one hundred eighty-seven clubs from across the state. It is believed to be the largest kids' state tournament in the nation.

"Dad was maybe not as knowledgeable about the sport compared to some of his coaching peers in terms of technique and training methods, but he was an organizer and promoter and used his connections to help grow the sport in Kansas. It is gratifying to see his legacy carrying on," said son Bill Knorr from his home in Silver Lake, Kansas in the fall of 2023.

Knorr's head coaching tenure at nineteen seasons was close to Patterson's twenty, the longest in K-State wrestling history. In addition to his coaching duties, he held the title of assistant athletic director and business manager for the athletic department.

Knorr was sixty-five years old when he passed away on September 9, 1972, while visiting relatives in Savannah, Missouri.

Bill Doyle – Class of 1932

Doyle's exploits as K-State's first and only NCAA champion and head coach of the first state champion high school team in Kansas are so compelling that he has a chapter of his own in this book. See *Bill Doyle, First and Only,* for his story.

Dick Fowler – Class of 1934

Fowler is only listed on the K-State roster during his senior year, 1933-34. He was also a member of the tennis team. The Holton native coached Colby to the state championship in 1936 in a tie for the title with perennial power Wichita East.

Dale Duncan – Class of 1938

Unsurprisingly, a St. Francis High School grad went on to success as a college wrestler and high school coach. The small northwest Kansas town is certainly a candidate for the "Wrestling Capital of Kansas" with a rich history that includes sixteen state championships.

Dale Duncan became the first state champion in school history when he won a state title during his senior year in 1934 at 135 pounds. He went on to qualify for the 1937 NCAAs at 145 pounds for the

Wildcats, where he went 1-1 at the championships held on the campus of Indiana State Teacher's College in Terre Haute.

Duncan coached at Oberlin, where he guided the Plainsmen to back-to-back state titles in 1942 and 1943.

Dale is part of a trio of brothers who qualified for the NCAAs for the Wildcats. Clifford qualified with him in 1937, and Glenn qualified in 1940 when the NCAAs were held at the University of Illinois in Champaign.

Leon "Red" Reynard – Class of 1940

Leon "Red" Reynard was a standout athlete at K-State before assuming the head coaching role for six years. *Photo Credit*: Collegiate Media Group.

Leon "Red" Reynard was born near Burr Oak in north central Kansas, but his family moved to Texas, and he entered the military service after graduating from Pharr San Juan Alamo High School in Texas in 1931.

He enrolled at K-State in the fall of 1936. When he finished in third place at 175 pounds at the 1940 NCAAs, he was already just months away from his twenty-seventh birthday.

By September 1941, he was back in the U.S. Army, serving until February 1946. In 1947, after longtime coach Buel "Pat" Patterson left for the University of Nebraska, Reynard began a six-year tenure as the Wildcat coach.

In August of 1953, he abruptly left his position at K-State to pursue a career as a car salesman.

Reynard's 1950-51 Wildcat team was the Big Seven Runner-up. He coached four individuals to conference titles and coached a pair of All-Americans (Charles Lyons and Ted Weaver).

Reynard passed away in 2008. He was ninety-four years old.

Warren "Barney" Boring – Class of 1947

FRONT ROW: Coach Boring

BACK ROW: Merlin Rueb, Robert Ackerman, Lee Mills, Paul Neville, Pete Gienger, Elmer Richers, Gordon Leonard, Dwane Raile, Don Stone

After leading St. Francis to three state titles (1949, 1952, and 1953), Warren Boring earned his doctorate from Indiana University. He then moved to California where he was on faculty at Long Beach State until his 1988 retirement. He was head wrestling coach of the 49ers from 1957-65. *Photo Credit*: St. Francis High School.

Warren Boring was part of the generation that got swept up in the WWII shutdown in college wrestling. He first enrolled at Kansas University in the fall of 1938 after graduating from Wyandotte High School, but after that program was disbanded, he took his talents to K-State, where he was on the team from 1939-41.

He served with distinction in WWII and returned to K-State when the program restarted after the war, graduating in the spring of 1947. He was captain of the 1946-47 team during Coach Buel Patterson's last season in Manhattan before moving on to the University of Nebraska.

Boring hailed from Kansas City, Kansas, but found himself on the opposite end of the state to begin his teaching and coaching career at

St. Francis High School. The Indians won state titles in 1949, 1952, and 1953 under his leadership.

Boring left Sainty in 1953 to pursue his doctorate in education at the University of Indiana, where he also helped coach the Hoosiers wrestling team. He earned his PhD in 1956.

After IU he headed west and joined the faculty of the physical education department at California State University, Long Beach. He also established the wrestling program there and served as head coach from 1957-65. He remained on the Long Beach faculty until his retirement in 1988.

Boring authored several articles on wrestling and published a book, *Science and Skill of Wrestling*, in 1975. He was an inaugural member of the Southern California Wrestling Association and served as the organization's president for ten years.

He was inducted into the Long Beach State University Athletic Hall of Fame in 1994 and the Kansas Wrestling Coaches Association Hall of Fame in 1998. The National Wrestling Hall of Fame, Kansas chapter, recognized him in 2003 with its Lifetime Service award after the California chapter recognized him in 2000.

Boring passed away in January 2007 at his home in Rossmoor, California, at the age of 87. He was survived by his wife of over five decades, Anne, and their five children.

Dave Winter – Class of 1955

Dave Winter enrolled at K-State after graduating from Savannah High School in Missouri. When his grades began to suffer, he dropped out and did a stint in the military before returning to complete his degree.

He took up wrestling for the first time in the military and continued during the 1954-55 season at K-State.

Winter began his teaching and coaching career at Claflin High School before making the move to Newton, which he adopted as his hometown after a nomadic existence during his formative years when his father was in the military.

While at Newton High, he led the Railers to the 1963 state title after knocking on the door with a runner-up finish in '62.

He moved to the collegiate level when he served as head coach at Fort Hays State University from 1963-70. After Fort Hays, he spent his remaining working years in the business sector. Winter was inducted into the Newton High School Athletic Hall of Fame in 2011. He passed away in 2015.

Bob Mancuso – Class of 1956

Bob Mancuso was an anomaly on the K-State roster in his era. He was one of the few who came from outside of the Sunflower State. Mancuso graduated from Omaha Central High School in 1951 and had an outstanding career at K-State.

He was also an anomaly as the only four-time NCAA qualifier in program history, participating in the 1952, 1953, 1954, and 1956 NCAA tournaments. This is not only impressive, but it is worth a fact-check.[6] During the 1951-52 season, the Big Seven allowed freshmen to compete in the conference tournament, which served as the NCAA qualifier. It is unclear, but this situation may have been an extension from the post-WWII exemption when the NCAA lifted the ban on freshmen competing at the varsity level. It wasn't until the 1972-73 school year that the freshman ban was permanently lifted[7].

Mancuso moved back to Omaha to start his teaching and coaching career. He led Bellevue High School to the 1961 state championship with five individual champions. After his short stay at Bellevue, he took his talents down the road to Lincoln.

From 1961-64 he coached in the college ranks, spending three seasons as head coach of the Nebraska Cornhuskers. His best season in Lincoln was 1961-62 when the team finished 9-2-1 in duals and in ninth place at the NCAA Championships with two individual All-Americans (Harold Thompson and Mike Nissen. He coached Nissen to an NCAA title in 1963).

Mancuso went into private business after coaching, where he successfully promoted and brought events to Omaha. The company,

Mid-America Expositions, is still a thriving business. Mancuso passed away in 2015 at the age of 81.

Kyle Mines – Class of 1957

Kyle Mines had several stops in his hall of fame coaching career, including a one-year stint as head coach at the University of Arizona.
Photo Credit: University of Arizona Special Collection.

Decatur Community High School in Oberlin produced two individual state champions in 1948 on its way to a fourth-place finish in the team standings. One of those state champions, senior 138-pounder Kyle Mines, also finished in third place at the 1946 state tournament.

In the spring of his senior year, he competed in a 1948 Olympic Trials qualifying event in Lincoln, Nebraska, where his only loss was to Lowell Lang, who was a three-time NCAA champion for Cornell College (Iowa) and a member of the 1947 NCAA champion team.[8]

After high school, Mines enrolled at K-State. He left after one year and ventured on a complicated path that brought him back to Manhattan five years later.

Kyle and his twin brother Keith were both freshmen on the K-State wrestling team during the 1948-49 season under Coach Red Reynard. Kyle also played baseball that year, when his coach was future head wrestling coach Fritz Knorr.

Keith married his high school sweetheart, Marilyn, and entered the military after his initial year at K-State, later returning to earn a degree in business. He went on to a successful career as an accountant. Keith and Marilyn had three children. He passed away in 2021.

Kyle enrolled in McCook Junior College in McCook, Nebraska, after his initial year in Manhattan. He joined the football team and was a standout lineman for the Indians. At the time, McCook did not have either a wrestling or baseball team.

His next move was to Denver, where he worked in construction. During this time, he got married to his girlfriend, Bonnie. While in Denver, they had their first child, Georganne. By 1951, the family moved back to McCook, Bonnie's hometown. They remained there until 1953. During this time, Kyle coached an age-group baseball team in McCook that competed for state-level honors.

The family moved to Manhattan, and Kyle re-enrolled at K-State and joined the wrestling team in the fall of 1953. This was Fritz Knorr's first year as head coach.

Mines was a twenty-three-year-old husband and father of a toddler, with another on the way (daughter Becky was born in 1954 in Manhattan). The family lived in married student housing on the K-State campus. A third daughter, Nancy, was born later. Despite the demands of his daily life, Mines competed at a high level and was a stalwart in the wrestling team's lineup. Bonnie worked as a secretary at the nearby Fort Riley military base.

Needing to earn an income and move on, he graduated after the fall semester of the 1956-57 school year, forgoing his senior wrestling season. He was awarded his teaching degree in January of 1957 and accepted a teaching and coaching position at Colby High School. Mines hit the ground running, leading the Eagles to the 1958 state championship. The title was the third for the Colby Eagle wrestling program.[9]

Mines then moved on to the college level when he became the head coach at the University of Arizona for one year. He also earned his master's degree during his time in Tucson.

That unbelievable progression from small-town western Kansas to the University of Arizona started a Hall of Fame career that eventually brought him back to his roots after high school teaching and/or coaching stops in Arizona, Colorado, Nebraska, Kansas, and Texas.

His next stop was South Mountain High School in Phoenix, where he remained for three years. Johnstown High School in Johnstown, Colorado, was starting a wrestling program, and Mines was hired to get it off on the right foot. He had a successful three years in north central Colorado before moving to the Nebraska panhandle community of Sydney.

Mines taught and coached at Sidney High School from 1965-71. The theme of short, but successful stays held true at SHS as he led the program to the 1970 state championship.

Early in 1971, Mines announced his resignation from Sidney High and contemplated retiring from coaching but remaining in education. His competitive fires, however, were reignited when a rival school from his high school days in the Northwest Kansas League came calling.

As of 2024, with its sixteen state titles, St. Francis ranks only behind Arkansas City (21) and Norton (17) in total number of championships. Mines' track record of success was enticing to St. Francis when it was in the market for a new coach.

He was at St. Francis from 1971-75 and led the Indians to two runner-up trophies, a third-place finish, and a sixth-place finish in four seasons. In 1975, St. Francis was the only school to capture more than one individual Grand State[10] championship when Perry Keller (167 pounds) and Les Zuege (unlimited) won titles.

St. Francis finished runner-up to Northwest Kansas League rival Oakley at the 1974 state tournament. The Plainsmen were led by fellow K-State grad Dale Samuelson, who just one year earlier was elevated to head coach at K-State from his grad assistant role.

After St. Francis, Mines embarked on a career in school administration, spending time at an elementary school in the Wheatfield school district and Deerfield High School before moving to Texas, where he finished his career in education as a teacher at Cal Farley Boys Ranch near Amarillo and later in the Harlingen Consolidated Independent School District in the far reaches of South

Texas.

Mines relocated to Oberlin, where he spent his retirement years. He was inducted into the Kansas Wrestling Coaches Association Hall of Fame in 2012.

In January 2018, the Decatur Community High School wrestling program awarded Kyle the "Spectator of the Year" award at a home dual in the DCHS gym. He rarely missed a home event and was touched by the gesture. He passed away in Oberlin on May 9, 2018, at the age of 87.

Kyle Mines (center) was awarded "Spectator of the Year" from the Decatur Community High School wrestling program in 2018 for his support of the team.
Photo Credit: Georganne Ishii personal collection.

Mines lived a colorful life with more than his share of rough patches. However, his motivation was the positive impact he had on the sport and the kids he coached.

He recited *The Athlete's Prayer* with his wrestlers before each competition. Found among his personal items after his death was Gayle Sayers' *I Am Third* poem.[11] His daughter Georganne Ishii reminisced about her father's influence from her California home. "One of the many sayings that he used to relay to kids was 'Make a Joyful Noise.' I believe that my father made a difference in every young athlete he coached and every student he taught. I believe he made a 'joyful noise' wherever he went. He was a very loving and caring man. He lived and breathed wrestling," she said.

Dee Gard – Class of 1961

Dee Gard coached Wichita Heights to state titles in 1968 and 1976.
The 1961 K-State grad was a two-time NCAA qualifier.
Photo Credit: Dee Gard personal collection.

Dee Gard graduated from Goodland High School in 1957 with three state medals, including a state championship as a sophomore. He then had a great career at K-State, where he qualified for the NCAA tournament at 147 pounds in both 1959 and 1960.

His Hall of Fame coaching career at Wichita Heights High School included state titles in 1968 and 1976. Gard also spent many years behind the whistle as a highly regarded official.

John Kadel was one of Coach Gard's prize pupils. The 1970 and 1971 state champion wrestled at Oklahoma University before transferring to K-State. "I had no experience with wrestling when I got to high school. Coach Gard was a sophomore football coach and invited me to go out for wrestling. The reputation of wrestling at Heights was strong, and Coach Gard was good at helping me to learn and motivating the team, although he was not a rah-rah guy. You came in and got to work," said Kadel. He added, "I didn't recognize his genius when I was in high school. I learned that when I was a coach myself. He believed in having the basics that you drilled and drilled. If he saw that you could do more, he added to it. He didn't yell and scream in the room or during competitions. It was all business with him. He's a great guy, and I learned a lot from him."

Gard spent his entire coaching career at Wichita Heights. "Something that stands out to me is that most of the wrestlers at Heights were blue-collar and knew what work was. They did what was expected of them," he said. As an example, he pointed to his first state championship team. "In '68, when we won state, Ark City hosted and was expected to win. We qualified five[12] and finished with two firsts, a second and two thirds. Those kids were special. All five of them were hard workers and did what was expected, which is not always true nowadays," he said.

After coaching, Gard moved into administration and began officiating. "I wanted to stay close to the sport. I enjoyed the camaraderie with the officials and coaches, and officiating gave me that opportunity," he said. He estimates that he worked 26 state tournaments. "I did have satisfaction in that I think I did a good job, some would argue differently (he said with a laugh), but my years in coaching, I really enjoyed that more," he said.

Gard was an inductee into the Kansas Wrestling Coaches Association Hall of Fame in 1999 and was recognized with the National Wrestling Hall of Fame's Lifetime Service to Wrestling award in 2004.

Gus Garcia – Class of 1964

Gus Garcia was coached by Bill Doyle at Douglass High School. He was a three-time NCAA qualifier at K-State and had a long, successful high school coaching career. He won a state title while coaching at Atwood High School in 1973.
Photo Credit: Collegiate Media Group.

Rosalio "Gus" Garcia was a state runner-up and fourth-place finisher by the time he graduated from tradition-rich Douglass High School in 1956, where he was coached by K-State legend Bill Doyle.

After a stint in the Marines, Garcia enrolled at K-State and qualified for the NCAA tournament in 1961, 1963, and 1964 at 130 pounds while competing for the Wildcats.

He went on to a long, distinguished high school coaching career with stops at Atwood and Augusta.

He led the Atwood Buffalos to twelve top ten state tournament finishes, including the 1973 state title. His 1977 team finished as state runner-up, and the 1971 and 1972 teams finished in third place in Class 2-1A.

At Augusta, seven teams finished in the top ten at state, including runner-up finishes in 1987 and 1988 in Class 4A.

All told, he coached eighty-three individuals to top four finishes at state. Included in that medal count are twenty-one state champions. His sons Gus, Jr. and Gabe accounted for six state medals, including a state title for Gus and a runner-up finish for Gabe. "He poured his whole life and soul into wrestling," said Gus, Jr. He added, "The success of my brother and I meant a lot to my dad. My title meant more to him than it did to me. It was a culmination of all of the hours and years investing the time in the sport, and to have that at the end was nice."

Garcia was inducted into the Kansas Wrestling Coaches Association Hall of Fame in 2000 and was honored with the National Wrestling Hall of Fame's Lifetime Service Award in 2004. In 2013, He was inducted into the Augusta High School Wrestling Hall of Fame as a charter member.

Garcia passed away at his home in Parsons in 2019. He was 80 years old.

Richard DeMoss – Class of 1965

Richard DeMoss graduated from Wellington High School in 1960. His coach,
Ken Spicher, and teammate Joe Seay also competed for K State. DeMoss
taught and coached in Kansas before moving to Oklahoma, where he led
Pawhuska High School to the 2A state championship in 1990.
John Smith appears in the photo presenting the championship plaque.
Photo Credit: Richard DeMoss personal collection.

Richard DeMoss graduated from Wellington High School in 1960, where he was a state runner-up in the 145-pound weight class in 1959 and a third-place finisher as a senior.

He followed teammate Joe Seay, a 1958 Wellington High grad, to K-State. Their high school coach, Ken Spicher, competed on the K-State wrestling team from 1952-55. His father, Richard DeMoss, Sr., also graduated from K-State, where he competed on the wrestling team during his freshman year, 1935-36.

DeMoss had a solid career for the Wildcats. He placed third in the 1965 Big Eight tournament in Norman at 157 pounds, which qualified him for the NCAA tournament held at the University of Wyoming. He went 2-1, winning his first two matches before falling to Iowa State's top seed, Gordon Hassman, in the quarterfinals. Hassman placed third but was upset in the semifinals, preventing DeMoss from entering the consolation bracket.

After graduating from K-State, he began a career as a Spanish teacher and wrestling coach. His first stop was four years at Rosedale High School in Kansas City, Kansas, and he spent another four years at Shawnee Mission Northwest High School.

Famed Oklahoma State wrestler and coach Myron Roderick (a Winfield, Kansas native) encouraged DeMoss to move to Oklahoma to continue his career in the classroom and on the mat. He had gotten to know Roderick during college and was invited by him to assist at camps and clinics and to get involved in wrestling association administrative work.

He accepted a position at Pawhuska High School in 1974 and remained there until his 2005 retirement. DeMoss led the Huskies to the 1990 Oklahoma 2A titles in both the dual and individual state tournaments.

The Oklahoma High School State tournament was held on the campus of OSU at Gallagher-Iba Arena in 1990, during Seay's time as head coach of the Cowboys. Unbeknownst to DeMoss, Seay hosted their high school coach for the weekend.

DeMoss' Huskies had a lock on the Class 2A crown, and Seay wanted to create a special moment for his former teammate after his first finalist won his individual title. Seay was waiting matside to congratulate DeMoss. Shielded from view was Coach Spicher, who appeared out of nowhere after Seay expressed his congrats. It was an emotional moment and something that DeMoss cherishes as one of the most memorable of his entire coaching career. Seay knew what it would mean to DeMoss and orchestrated the whole thing. "It was overwhelming. I was laughing and bawling at the same time," said DeMoss some thirty-four years later.

DeMoss contributes much of his success to the opportunities he had through the connections he has made. "Myron [Roderick] gave me opportunities and the best education in coaching that I could have had. He took me under his wing and introduced me to many of the top names in the sport to learn alongside," he said.

DeMoss continues to live in Pawhuska with his wife, Delores. The couple celebrated their fifty-eighth wedding anniversary in August 2024.

He continues to follow the sport and is appreciative of his career. "I never expected to be a teacher and coach, but I'm glad I chose that path. It was a fulfilling career," he said.

Jerry Cheynet – Class of 1966

After earning All-American honors in 1966, Jerry Cheynet coached at Oakley High School.
He then started the program at Lake Superior State University and finished his career at
Virginia Tech, where he spent twenty-two seasons as head coach.
Photo Credit: Virgina Tech Athletics.

Jerry Cheynet arrived on the K-State campus in the fall of 1960 after graduating from Wichita Southeast High School.

He took a circuitous path to earning his college degree six years later. After struggling in pre-veterinary classes during his freshman year, he returned to Wichita to work for Boeing before re-enrolling at K-State in the fall of 1962.

Interestingly, when he returned, Cheynet was again classified as a freshman and subject to the freshman eligibility rule, which meant that he would have to wait another year to compete for the Wildcats, a distance of four years since he last competed on the mat as a high school senior.

When he entered the lineup, he never looked back and put together one of the best careers in program history. He became an NCAA All-American during his senior season when he placed sixth at 137 pounds at the 1966 NCAA Championships held on the campus of Iowa State University in Ames, Iowa.

After earning his undergraduate degree, Cheynet spent a year as a graduate assistant under Fritz Knorr. With his master's degree in hand, he accepted a teaching and head wrestling position at Oakley

High School, where he remained for two years.

His goal was always to get into college coaching. He learned of a position at Lake Superior State University in Sault Sainte Marie, Michigan, through a recruiting service. The school was adding a wrestling program, and Cheynet was offered the position.

From 1969-74 he made his home in Michigan's Upper Peninsula near the Canadian border. During that time, he built the LSSU program into a winner. His 42-8-2 dual record included an undefeated 1972-73 season when the Lakers went 13-0. The team also won three NAIA District titles and finished in the top twenty of the NAIA nationals during each of Cheynet's last four years. The team also claimed the first Great Lakes Intercollegiate Athletic Conference (GLIAC) title in 1973.

After the 1973-74 season, it was time to move on. Cheynet's successor would be star pupil and newly-graduated Jim Fallis. The twenty-one-year-old was a four-time NAIA All-American and two-time national champion in the 158-pound weight class in 1973 and 1974. As a senior, Fallis was also part of history when LSSU dual-affiliated with NCAA Division III. The first DIII tournament was held at Wilkes University in Wilkes-Barre, Pennsylvania, March 1-2, 1974. Fallis won the 158-pound title, was named Outstanding Wrestler, and won the Gregorian Award (most falls in the least amount of time) at the tournament.

Fallis coached for twelve years at LSSU, followed by a distinguished career as an athletic director at his alma mater, Northern Colorado University, and Northern Arizona University. Cheynet remembers Fallis for his great work ethic and focus. Fallis credits his mentor with preparing him long-term for the career ahead of him.

"His demeanor is what I remember. He was never too high or too low. He was very balanced in his approach. He was always a positive motivator. I have to admit, I wasn't always the best of teammates. He would remain positive, but he would pull me aside, and he'd tell me, 'I'm really disappointed in how you handled this and that.' At the moment it never impacts you the way it does later on. I reflected back on those situations when I was coaching and maybe even more so when I was an athletic director. He had a lot of impact later on in life that didn't necessarily register in the moment," said Fallis.

In addition to Cheynet's duties as head wrestling coach at Lake Superior, he also served as head golf coach and head cross country coach. This mixture was uncommon then at the college level and unheard of in today's year-round commitment for each sport.

In the fall of 1974, Cheynet began an association with Virginia Tech Athletics, which continues to this day. As of March 2024, Cheynet is still listed as operations coordinator for the men's soccer team. You read that correctly, Cheynet not only served as head coach of the wrestling program from 1974-96 but also head men's soccer coach from 1974-01. And, not to be outdone by his three-sport commitment at Lake Superior State, Cheynet was head coach for *four* different sports while at Virginia Tech. In addition to wrestling and men's soccer, he was head coach of men's golf (1980-83) and women's soccer (2002).

When he took over the wrestling program, Tech was at a disadvantage, with only four scholarships when fully-funded programs were allotted 9.9.

The school's profile wasn't what it is today. The Hokies weren't in a wrestling conference. They competed in the generic Eastern Regional along with other schools not affiliated with a conference qualifier (this was before conference "affiliate membership" was allowed).

Things went from bad to worse in the 1980-81 school year. Due to funding issues, wrestling and field hockey were on the chopping block. Wrestling was spared, but the already-limited scholarships were completely eliminated. It wouldn't be until 1989 that scholarships would return, and then back to the original scanty four full rides to divide among a team of around thirty.

Ironically, football lobbied for retaining scholarships for the wrestling program, but with a catch.

Bill Dooley was the head football coach at Virginia Tech from 1978 to 1986. He liked to use wrestling as a recruiting tool to attract linemen—and siphon scholarship dollars away from wrestling to football. The practice caught up with him and contributed to his being relieved of his duties in 1986 during an NCAA investigation. It wasn't until Tom Brands arrived in 2004 that Tech became a fully-funded wrestling program.

In 1996, VT Athletic Director David Braine approached Coach Cheynet and asked him to choose between wrestling and soccer. In the modern era of the time commitment of big-time college athletics, serving as head coach of two sports teams was impractical.

Many were surprised by his choice of soccer, but Cheynet decided based on his age and the stability of the programs. He was in his mid-50s and less able to handle the physical demands of wrestling. Further, when comparing the financial health of the two programs, soccer's trajectory was going in a better direction than wrestling's.

He remained in the head men's soccer role for five more seasons, then stepped into the head woman's role when an interim need arose.

Beyond playing intramural soccer at K-State, Cheynet never played four of the five sports that he coached at the college level. At Wichita Southeast, he participated in wrestling all four years, track on a limited basis, and was a backup catcher on the JV baseball team for a season. He points to his willingness to learn as the key to taking on the learning curve. Regarding soccer, he pointed out that in the 1970s, the sport was just gaining popularity, and coaches were in short supply. "A lot of college programs had inexperienced coaches," he said.

It was interesting to learn that he was not sought out for the K-State opening after Fritz Knorr passed away in 1972 or when Fred Fozzard was dismissed in 1975. He believes that to be the case for Joe Seay, as well. "Kansas State did not touch base with me either time. They got a good coach in there with Fozzard," said Cheynet. He added, "Nationally, around that time, with Title IX, there were a lot of programs being dropped, so the situation around K-State wasn't that unusual."

Title IX was enacted on June 23, 1972. We will discuss Title IX in more depth in the final chapter of this book, but it does appear that Cheynet has a valid point about the times wrestling was living in during the demise of the sport at K-State.

Cheynet points to the program's survival as a major accomplishment when reflecting on his career at Tech. Competing with the limited funding and low profile of a program not even affiliated with a conference was very difficult. Today, in contrast, Tech's wrestling program is fully funded and competes in the Atlantic Coast Conference (ACC).

Current Iowa State University head coach, Kevin Dresser, coached at Virginia Tech from 2006-17. He first came to know Cheynet during his time as a coach at Christiansburg High School, located just minutes from the VA Tech campus.

Dresser reflects on Cheynet and his influence on him, "He was the men's Division I soccer coach and the head Division I men's wrestling coach at the same time, so you think how hard that is just right there. I'm sure it saved them money, and it allowed them to keep both programs when they probably were struggling in the '70s and '80s. Now look, their sports are doing really really well. Their wrestling program is good, and their soccer programs are good. What a great guy. His positivity is just off the charts. He is just such an upbeat, positive guy and that's infectious."

Current Virginia Tech coach, Tony Robie, has the Hokies competing at a high level. He can attract the nation's most talented recruits with the program's funding, status, and success. Cheynet can look on with pride in holding it together when times were tough in Blacksburg. Coach Cheynet's influence isn't lost on Robie, "First of all Jerry is a very high character human being, and he brought good people in, good high character people into Virginia Tech. Everyone you talk to that knows Jerry Cheynet, or that wrestled for Jerry Cheynet, just says great things about him. I think that's the biggest thing, is that he built relationships. He branded wrestling in a positive way at Verginia Tech during his tenure there and that has carried on. He's definitely a big part of the history of the program."

Marvin Landes – Class of 1969

Due to the coaching success that K-State wrestling grads achieved, the standard was set high for inclusion in this chapter. Winning a State title or coaching at the highest level of college wrestling is a high bar, but it is necessary to keep the pages in this chapter to a reasonable number.

Marvin Landes didn't lead the Garden City Buffalos to a state championship during his short time as head coach, but he came close and had a short but impressive run in southwest Kansas—so impressive that the criteria for his inclusion was bent.

After graduating from Wellington High School, Landes made his way to Stillwater, where he spent a year at OSU. After transferring to Kansas State, he became a regular in the lineup in the 130-pound weight class for the Wildcats.

After starting the junior high program at Chapman, he took the head coaching position at Garden City High School, where he hit the ground running. During his first season, in 1972-73, the Buffalos went 8-0 in duals and finished as 4A state runner-up. The Buffs fell just 2.5 points shy of champion Newton, led by Hall of Famer Delbert Erickson.

It was much of the same in 1974 when Garden was again runner-up to Newton after a 7-0 dual season. In year three, his team finished in third place at the 1975 4A state tournament after another 7-0 season.

With plans to return to K-State to further his education derailed, he took back the resignation that he submitted and coached for one more year. The team had another solid season, finishing in seventh place at state with a 6-1-2 dual record. Interestingly, the two ties were against Liberal, and the loss was across the border to Lamar High School in Colorado.

Landes remained in Garden City but gave up coaching at the high school. He put his energies into teaching, officiating, and helping build the Garden City youth wrestling program.

Dale Samuelson – Class of 1972

Before Dale Samuelson became head coach at K-State, he was a standout for the Wildcats. He was a two-time NJCAA All-American for Colby Community College before enrolling at K-State. *Photo Credit. Collegiate Media Group.*

As a senior for Oakley High, Dale Samuelson finished his high school career as state runner-up at 127 pounds in 1968.

In the fall of 1967, Colby Community College announced the start of its wrestling program under Vic Oelke's leadership. After the initial season, Oelke moved into the athletic director role, and Gary "Pudge" Wilson became head coach.

Wilson was a Colorado native with an outstanding college career at the University of Northern Colorado. Prior to his junior college post at Colby, he was head coach at St. Francis. The 1966 Kansas High School Coach of the Year, he led the Indians to state titles in 1966 and 1967.

The Colby Community College Trojans were a team largely made up of athletes from the wrestling-rich communities of the Northwest Kansas League, of which Colby High School was a part. The team would now be coached by a former high school coach from the school with the deepest tradition among those communities. Samuelson saw the appeal and enrolled in the fall of 1968.

He became the first All-American in the program's history when he finished in fourth place at the 1969 National Junior College Athletic Association (NJCAA) national tournament at 137 pounds. A year later, he equaled that placing at 134 pounds. Samuelson's junior college success led him to Kansas State University, where he finished his college career.

He competed for K-State from 1970-72 and was a two-year starter and NCAA qualifier at 142 pounds as a senior after placing fourth at the Big Eight tournament.

Only six months after wrestling his final college match in College Park, Maryland, at the NCAA tournament, he was thrust into the head coach position for the Wildcats after the death of Fritz Knorr in September of 1972. Samuelson graduated in May and was settling into a graduate assistant position. If not for the whistle around his neck in the team pictures, one would assume that he was one of the athletes.

After the 1972-73 season, Samuelson applied for the job when it was posted, but Athletic Director Ernie Barrett opted for the more experienced and accomplished Fred Fozzard. Samuelson returned to his hometown and had a long and successful teaching and coaching career at Oakley High. Less than a year after leaving Manhattan, he led his alma mater to the 1974 state title in Class 2-1A. All told, fourteen of his teams finished in the top 5 at state, including the title team and two runner-up teams.

Samuelson was inducted into the Kansas Wrestling Coaches Association Hall of Fame in 2006. He passed away in 2017.

Wayne Jackson – Class of 1974

Wayne Jackson (right) accumulated thirteen state titles at Ark City with friend and assistant coach, Mark Richardson, at his side for all of them. *Photo Credit*: Wayne Jackson personal collection.

This chapter's final entry profiles the second best-known coach in the group, behind the chapter's namesake and first entry, Joe Seay.

Anyone in the know in Kansas wrestling circles has Wayne Jackson on their short list of greatest high school wrestling coaches in Kansas history, with a record thirteen state titles,[13] all at Arkansas City High School.

Jackson's parents, Carl and Mary, had Oklahoma roots before moving north, first to Syracuse in southwest Kansas, then to Ark City.

His dad was a successful educator and coach at Newkirk High School in Oklahoma and Syracuse High before moving to Ark City[14] in 1954. He coached basketball, track and field, and football along the way, but he was known mostly as a highly regarded football coach who brought a new level of success to each stop.

Before his coaching days, the elder Jackson played center for Oklahoma State and was part of the 1945 Sugar Bowl team that beat St. Mary's of California 33-13.

In late August 1964, Carl Lee Jackson died of a heart attack. He was only thirty-nine years old. He left his wife and four children, including the oldest, thirteen-year-old Wayne.

Looking back, Wayne acknowledges the Ark City community, especially coaches, for rallying around him and his family during that difficult time. "The coaches and the whole Ark City community helped me and my family through that tough time. It was hard on everybody. It was so sudden. Coach [Bunt] Speer was a good friend of my dad's, and he was a big help," said Jackson.

Wayne was born in Newkirk but is as Ark City as Ark City. He grew up there and graduated from ACHS in 1969. He was a three-time state wrestling medalist and two-time runner-up for the Bulldogs, who were state champions during his freshman and senior seasons under the leadership of head coach Speer.[15] Ask him about his high school career, and he will likely start by telling you that he "never won anything."

Put him in a room full of accomplished coaches and ask an unknowing bystander to pick out the one with thirteen state titles to his credit. Jackson may be the last guess. The bystander may be more apt to label him the custodian who knows where the best local fishing hole can be found rather than being the alpha of the room. He is humble, genuine, and plain-spoken. His awe-shucks persona is the immediate and lasting impression.

Even his fashion speaks to his personality. During his coaching days it was blue jeans and the well-worn satin jacket emblazoned with the same "ARK CITY" block letters on the front that decorated the front of the Bulldog singlets. Tough, no-nonsense.

Spend a little time with him, and you will begin to understand. He has that "something" that can be neither taught nor dissected. Only generational coaches have it.

When the weathered, 5' 6", 170-pound coach speaks to you, you are both in awe and feel that you are talking to an old friend who enjoys your company as much as you enjoy his. Kids would run through a brick wall for him. He gave opposing coaches ulcers, but they respected him and considered him their friend. He has the rare quality of being a driven competitor and also a genuine good guy.

Jackson was a star at K-State. He completed his career as a three-time NCAA qualifier, joining only four other Wildcats with that distinction[16]. After his college career, he dabbled in freestyle and competed in a 1976 Olympic Trials regional qualifier held in Farmington, New Mexico,[17] but he was more interested in leaving the wrestling shoes in the center of the mat[18] and entering the coaching ranks.

He began his teaching and coaching career at Jay Shideler Junior High[19] in Topeka, where he remained for one year. He moved back to Arkansas City in 1976 and hasn't left. He served as an assistant coach at ACHS from 1976-78. In 1978, Jackson took over as head coach at his alma mater, and the rest is history.

He won his first state title in 1982 and his last in 2000. In 2004, he unretired for two seasons and showed that he still had what it took to keep the program on track with two top-ten finishes at State, including the '05 team that brought home a runner-up trophy.

Ark City's success under Jackson's leadership is jaw-dropping. Thirteen state titles, five runner-up finishes, four third-place finishes, and only two teams that did not bring a trophy home from state in twenty-four seasons.[20]

At the height of its success, Ark City put together a string of eleven state titles in a row. During the midpoint of that run, they had a formidable foe nipping at their heels. Salina South had teams that could challenge the Bulldogs. Some consider Ark City and South to be the top two teams in the entire state regardless of class in 1993 and 1994. South was loaded; Ark City found a way.

Salina South was led by head coach Bob Warkentine.[21] The Cougars were ranked #1 coming into the state tournament in 1994. That was a bold prediction considering that Ark City had won the last six in a row (and would win the next five), but it was a founded prediction based on how South was running through the competition. In the end, it was Ark City by 37.5 points. South would have to settle for a runner-up finish for the second year in a row. There was no consolation prize, but South's 152.5 points were twenty-seven points higher than the next highest team champion from the other three classifications.

After the '94 tournament ended, Jackson was quoted as saying, "It's always fun to win state, but beating Salina South makes it even better. South is a good team and they'd be tops in almost any other state. Our streak is going to end sometime, but I'm glad it wasn't this year because we had an awful good team too."[22]

Thirty years later, Warkentine remembers the rivalry well and reflects fondly on Jackson. "Wayne Jackson is an incredible person. I feel fortunate to have coached in an era with Duwane Miller[23] and Wayne Jackson. They are iconic in the history of Kansas wrestling. I was honored to go through at the same time as those two and fortunate that we had some teams that could compete with them."

Warkentine was impressed with how Jackson handled himself during competitions. "With Wayne, it was incredible how calm and collected he was in the corner. He seemed to rarely get out of his chair. The way he saw it was that his coaching was done in the room. He never seemed to stress or get angry," said Warkentine.

Warkentine can't put a finger on the reason for the avalanche of success during the Jackson years at Ark City but thinks a factor that can't be dismissed is that the coach and town represent the tradition of the midwestern work ethic and "toughness without flamboyance."

Warkentine, who himself hails from southeast Kansas, attended Cowley County Community College in Ark City after graduating from Wellington High in 1972. Like most small-town rivalries, he grew up despising the Ark City Bulldogs, who were less than an hour away in the school's big yellow bus.

As a coach, he attempted to take a page from Jackson's playbook. During a time when athletic clothing manufacturers were beginning to turn out more modernized and eye-catching warm-ups, Jackson never allowed Ark City to waiver from its signature purple or gold hoodie decorated with simple block lettering in the opposite color.[24] Warkentine, seeing the fashion statement as an ingredient to their success, actually discarded his team's fancy new duds and went basic, copying the leaders with a simple hooded sweatshirt and plain lettering of his own. The legacy of Coach Jackson in the actions of his adversary!

Fellow K-State wrestler, Dennis Switzky, was part of the incoming Wildcat Class of 1969 that included Jackson. He remembers the 134-pounder as a tenacious competitor and wasn't surprised by his coaching success. "I was not near Wayne's weight class, so I didn't work out with him, but I do remember his duck under. He could hit that on about anyone." He added, "We used to kid him about his 'Ark City accent.'"

That regional dialect is part of who he is, and Switzky believes a clue to his success. "I was not surprised [by his success]. He started his career in Topeka, but I don't think it was a good fit for him. When he moved back to Ark City, he was around his people and his environment. It was a good fit, and the results showed it." Switzky added a line common when asking a fellow coach about Jackson, "Wayne was always a good guy. That's how I remember him during my time coaching against him."

Switzky spent thirty-two years at Topeka-Seaman High School and another eight years at Royal Valley. During his time at Seaman, his Vikings competed in the same classification as the Bulldogs. In 1995, Seaman was third in the state behind Ark City and runner-up Kapaun Mt. Carmel, who was coached by Duwane Miller. For Switzky, going toe to toe with two of the most iconic programs and coaches in the history of Kansas wrestling was just part of the task. "At the time, I didn't think much of it. I was surprised that we did as well as we did and finished that high. The awareness is so much greater now than it was then. We didn't see those teams until state, so we really didn't know what to expect," he said.

Arkansas City Mayor Chad Beeson was a three-time state champion at Ark City High from 1989-91. He recalls the routine and intensity of practice sessions under Coach Jackson. "It was a competitive and deep room where a state champion would occasionally get put on his back by a JV wrestler," he said. The practice routine was such that over three decades later, Beeson can still blurt out, "Single Leg, Double Leg, High Crotch, Duckunder, Duckunder, Arm Drag, Arm Drag" in quick succession when recalling the sequence of the "Scarecrow" drill. The weekly regime was also predictable, from Monday's challenge matches to weekend competitions.

Technical instruction—large-group demonstrations followed by guided and independent practice, then regrouping to work out the kinks—is common in wrestling rooms across the nation, but not in Jackson's Ark City room. "We drilled a lot, and Coach would fix technical problems on the spot during live wrestling. Our focus seemed to be more on toughness and grit rather than technique. I can't really explain it, but he had a way of getting the best out of his wrestlers," said Beeson.

Beeson's son, Jake, was a four-time state medalist and two-time champion who captured a national title while wrestling for Pratt Community College.[25]

When Jackson had coached long enough for sons of his wrestlers to start appearing at the Ark City Takedown Club youth practices, the kids were in awe when they finally got to meet the coach that their fathers talked about in such glowing terms.

When Jake, now in his twenties, gets a call from Coach Jackson, "The Living Legend" appears on his phone's screen. Jackson, of course, would be embarrassed to hear this, but the message is clear: Wayne Jackson's influence in the Ark City wrestling community is like that pebble making ripples on the water.

The story of Jackson's coaching lore would not be complete without mention of his right-hand man, Mark Richardson. Coach Richardson, who passed away in 2020, was coaching at the junior high in Ark City for a few years before Jackson arrived and then served as his assistant from 1979 until Jackson's retirement in 2000.

Richardson stayed on in the assistant role when Greg Buckbee assumed head coaching duties and helped the Bulldogs collect another state title in 2003.

"Nobody will really know the role that Coach Richardson played in the success of Jackson's career. I'm not sure we would have had the success that we did without him," said Beeson, who points to Richardson's behind-the-scenes help from compiling statistics to doing inventory to making sure paperwork was in order, as essential to giving the singularity-focused Jackson the ability to develop athletes and win titles.

Richardson was also more than just the in-season assistant to Jackson. The two were friends off the mat, spending time socializing and fishing and hunting in the great outdoors. "I couldn't have done it without him. He was good at doing the organizing and administrative things that I wasn't good at. He was also able to connect with some of the kids better than I was," said Jackson. He added, "We did a lot away from wrestling too. We fished a lot. We also started into the cattle business together and were sometimes working with that until 8 or 9 o'clock after practice."

Records are made to be broken, but we may never see Wayne Jackson's accomplishments surpassed. His statistics and trophy collection will reflect well on history, but to him, the focus remains steadfast on the kids.

"Wrestling builds so many things you need in life. It's a great sport and it's helped every kid that has wrestled at Ark City. It has made them better people. I don't want a legacy for myself, but a legacy for Ark City wrestling and Ark City kids, that wrestling and the program have helped them be better people and lead better lives. That's what I hope," he said.

Chapter Six Endnotes: *LegaSeay*

1. Interesting side note: the 1963 tournament was the first that placed out to six, a system that was in place through the 1978 tournament. In the early years only the top three were designated as All-Americans (1928-1935). From 1936-1962, All-American status was awarded to the top four place winners. In 1979, All-American status was expanded to the top eight in each weight class, which continues to be the case as of 2024.
2. A 3-0 win over Lee Deitrick of Michigan in the first round and by fall in overtime against Penn State's George Edwards in the next round.
3. The blood round is a term used to signify the match in the consolation bracket where the winner is guaranteed All-American status and the loser's tournament ends and is out of contention for All-American honors. "Heartbeat Round" and "Round of 12" are also common terms used to signify this important round in the tournament.
4. Freestyle and Greco-Roman are the styles of wrestling that are contested on the international level and at the Olympics. "Folkstyle" (also called collegiate style) is the style common in the United States from the youth through college ages. Folkstyle is unique to the United States.
5. The exact history of this dual participation and qualifying criteria is a bit vague, but 1992 was the final year for dual participation and only for those grandfathered in.
6. Mancuso's NCAA tournament log: 1952 (2-2 at 123 pounds), 1953 (1-2 at 123 pounds), 1954 (0-1 at 130 pounds), 1956 (1-1 at 130 pounds).
7. In January 1972, the NCAA voted to lift the ban on freshmen competing on the varsity level, starting with the 1972-73 school year. It was the first time since the Korean War that the ban on freshmen had been lifted. The decision remains unimpeded to this day.
8. Read *The Dream Team of 1947* by Arno Paul Niemand for a fascinating look at Cornell's NCAA champion team. No other private school before or since has won the NCAA wrestling team title.
9. The program now has six titles under the direction of five different coaches, with the latest title coming in 2016.
10. Grand State was a unique KSHSAA-sponsored event that was contested for only two years, 1975 and 1976. It was an all-class tournament held the week after the individual class state tournaments. Brackets were made up of the top four finishers from each of the four classifications. Both tournaments were held at Gross Coliseum on the campus of Ft. Hays State College. Girls' basketball and wrestling were the only sports that held Grand State tournaments both years. Boys' basketball was added in 1976.
11. Sayers, who played football at Kansas University before becoming the great Chicago Bears running back, titled his 1972 biography, *I am Third.*
12. Doug Lunt (127 pounds) and brother Bob (133) were the champions. Wardell Bell (138) was runner-up. Bob Ledbetter (103) and Bill Jabara (120) finished in third place. Doug Lunt went on to wrestle at Iowa State. Bob Lunt competed for the University of Alabama, which had wrestling at the time.

13. After the completion of the 2025 KSHSAA State Tournament, Brett Means of Goddard is tied with Wayne Jackson with 13 State titles. Norton's Billy Johnson is next with 11.

14. Carl Jackson was at Newkirk High School from 1947-52, Syracuse from 1952-54, and Ark City from 1954 until his death in 1964.

15. Speer, a 1939 graduate of K-State, was the first wrestling coach in the storied history of Ark City. Only four years after establishing the program, the Bulldogs won the 1964 state title. Speer led the program to four state titles (1964, 1966, 1969, 1970). He also served as football coach at ACHS and is a member of the Cowley County Community College Hall of Fame for his accomplishments there. He coached football, basketball, track, and golf at what was then called Arkansas City Junior College before his time at Ark City High.

16. The other three-time NCAA qualifiers include: Gary Haller (1956-58), Joe Seay (1961-63), Gus Garcia (1961, 1963-64), and Ron Tacha (1969-71). Bob Mancuso is the only four-time NCAA qualifier in K-State history (1952-54, 1956). Read more about Jackson's college career in this book's final chapter, "I am Woman, Hear me Roar!"

17. Gary Blosser, Jody Thompson, and an unidentified wrestler were part of the group that competed. Blosser won the competition to qualify for the next phase of the qualifying process.

18. The sport of wrestling has a long-held tradition of signifying retirement from competing. After the referee has raised the hand of the winner, the retiree remains in the center of the mat. Shoes are removed and placed in the center of the mat, the crowd acknowledges the emotional wrestler, who waves farewell and walks off the mat.

19. Jay Shideler Junior High is now Jay Shideler Elementary in the Auburn-Washburn school district in Topeka.

20. The Bulldogs finished in fourth place in 1981 and in eighth place at Jackson's final state tournament in 2006.

21. Warkentine was inducted into the state chapter of the National Wrestling Hall of Fame in 2008 for Lifetime Service and the Kansas Wrestling Coaches Hall of Fame in 2013. He was also a head football coach during his career, but it was in the sport of tennis that he has the most coaching accolades. He retired from coaching in 2018 after six years as head coach of both mens' and womens' programs at Kansas Wesleyan University. While at Salina Central High School, he coached five state championship teams. In 2009, he was inducted into the Kansas Tennis Coaches Association Hall of Fame.

22. *The Salina Journal*, February 28, 1994, p. 11.

23. Duwane Miller, 1961 NCAA champion for Oklahoma University, coached at Douglass High School before two stints at Kapaun Mt. Carmel Catholic High School in Wichita. He is one of the all-time coaching greats in Kansas with eight state championships and the only two Grand State championships in Kansas history.

24. To be clear, there was no choice of sweatshirt color for the wearer. Depending on the season, it was only purple or gold. During your four-year-stay in high school, you may have accumulated only one color, depending on the season the switch was made.

25. Jake Beeson was NJCAA national champion for Pratt Community College in 2020 at 149 pounds. He finished as runner-up at 149 pounds in both 2021 and 2022.

-7-
"Going my way?"

The slow boil of the K-State wrestling program's demise heated up in March 1973, with the tipping point being an administrative decision not to fund the trip to the NCAA championships.

Three Wildcats qualified based on their top four finishes at the Big Eight tournament in Columbia, Missouri, which served as the NCAA championships qualifier. Fourth-place finishers Roger Fisher (118 pounds) and 190-pounder Gary Walter took the news hard but accepted their fate.

Then there was K-State's 134-pounder. The whole situation might have gone quietly unnoticed, at least to the general sports enthusiast, if not for an unlikely rebel named Wayne Jackson.

Jackson, whose outstanding coaching career is detailed in the previous chapter, "LegaSeay," finished in third place at the Big Eight tournament behind champion Bobby Stites (Oklahoma State) and runner-up Bill Fjetland (Iowa State). Both became All-Americans at the '73 NCAAs when Stites finished as runner-up and Fjetland in fourth place.

The directive from Coach Dale Samuelson via Athletic Director Ernie Barrett hit Jackson like a ton of bricks. The reason given for the lack of support for the trip to nationals was that none of the trio finished as champions in their weight class at the Big Eight tournament. The administration pointed to an "athletic department policy" established by Barrett, which stated that K-State would not send wrestlers to a national tournament unless they finished in first place in their weight class at the qualifier. The policy was said to be similar to one used for track and field. However, one has to wonder if Barrett knew that just a year earlier Jackson had qualified for the NCAAs and competed at the event on the campus of the University of Maryland in College Park after earning his spot with a fourth-place finish at the Big Eight tournament.

The news was delivered unceremoniously in the days after the team returned from Columbia. Attempts to meet with the administration to reverse the decision and find a way to fund the trip fell on deaf ears. Assistant director of athletics and business manager, Hindman Wall, relayed that the decision was final and a meeting was not necessary.

Jackson was pinned in the opening round of the 1972 NCAAs and based on his opponent's failure to advance to the semifinals, did not have the opportunity to compete in the consolation bracket. With that experience behind him, he was motivated and poised for an All-American run at the '73 tournament. "I had a good season going and thought I had a shot. I wanted to improve on what I did at nationals the year before," said Jackson.

Before detailing Jackson's next move, some context is in order. Coach Samuelson was twenty-two years old. After a stint at Colby Community College, he finished his athletic career and undergraduate studies at K-State two years later. He was a teammate of Jackson (and future brother-in-law), who also qualified for the '72 nationals.[1]

Fritz Knorr preceded Samuelson as head coach. Knorr had an association with K-State that went back to 1927 when he enrolled as a freshman. He was head wrestling coach for nineteen seasons and associate athletic director when he died in September 1972. Graduate assistant Samuelson was named head coach by default. As previously mentioned, he was just six months removed from his undergraduate studies and was a teammate to most of the student-athletes who were now his charges.

Samuelson didn't have the know-how or clout to fight the decision. Barrett was a star basketball player who led the Wildcats to the NCAA championship game in 1951 and played for the Boston Celtics before returning to Manhattan to serve as a coach and then enter athletic administration. Samuelson was an unknown, while Barrett was already known as "Mr. K-State," a moniker he would carry for the rest of his life. A larger-than-life statue of Barrett, who passed away in 2023 at the age of 93, stands near the west entrance to

Bramlage Coliseum on the K-State campus. The wrestling program was a sitting duck.

Jackson, a plain-spoken, salt-of-the-earth type, earned the right to compete at the nationals and come hell or high water, he was going! After Samuelson dropped the news and the administration refused to compromise, he hatched a plan to hitchhike to the nationals. He tried to convince Fisher and Walter to join in, but they wouldn't bite. He also informed Hindman Wall of his intentions.

Jackon's simple, uncomplicated plan to hitchhike to nationals was not bad for a cheap ride to Topeka, an hour's journey east on I-70, or a three-hour trek to his stomping grounds in southeast Kansas. But the '73 NCAAs were at the University of Washington, in Seattle! That's two time zones and 1,800 miles of plains, mountains, and forests away from the Flint Hills of Manhattan, Kansas. Jackson had little experience thumbing it. "I might have hitchhiked to Newkirk a time or two when I was in high school, but that's about it," said Jackson. Newkirk, Oklahoma, is less than twenty miles south of his childhood home in Arkansas City.

Somewhere in the vicinity of where Wayne Jackson was let off on the outskirts of Manhattan in March 1973 to begin his journey to Seattle, as it looks in the summer of 2024. *Photo by the author.*

If there is a story that defines a person, it's Wayne Jackson and his trip to nationals. His straightforward rationale? "I just wanted to rassle." He wasn't playing politics, making a statement, or checking off a bucket list item. He just wanted to "rassle!" The last thing he wanted to do was cause a stir but cause a stir he did.

The Big Eight tournament concluded on Saturday, February 24, 1973. The trio of qualifiers was informed that they wouldn't be going to nationals a few days later. With $70 in his pocket, Jackson's adventure started when a friend and teammate, Eric Hilding, drove him to the outskirts of Manhattan and let him out on Thursday morning, March 1st. The NCAA tournament was slated for March 8-10.

The adventure started off less than smooth. Steps into the journey, he was confronted by an angry dog. A short ride of about a mile on Highway 24 followed. He was on his way after a truck driver then took him to Lincoln, Nebraska, one hundred forty miles north of Manhattan, before making his way to Nebraska's panhandle after a few more rides.

The story is legendary in the K-State wrestling community, and a little spice has been added for effect over the years. Because the errant detail made it into the papers, the most prominent myth is that Jackson stayed the night in jail in the western Nebraska community of Ogallala.

He did, in fact, have an overnight stay in Ogallala after being dropped there. The town cops assisted him, but a scene with Otis from the *Andy Griffith Show* it was not. The officers saw him wandering their jurisdiction late at night and offered to help. Jackson asked to stay in the local jail. With a chuckle, the officers let him know that wasn't allowed and helped find him a room at a local hotel.

He paid $2.00 for the night in "this ratty motel." The accommodations were sparse but included a television. He recalls passing the night watching coverage of the occupation of Wounded Knee, South Dakota. The night in the motel also marked the only overnight stay in his epic journey.

For a long stretch that included passing through Green River, Wyoming, Jackson hopped in with a character named Howard J. Tickle, who was in the business of driving vehicles from one dealership to another, oftentimes over long distances. During this leg of the journey, both driver and passenger were given a citation from the Wyoming Highway Patrol for "stopping on an interstate highway for reasons other than an emergency" and hitchhiking. Jackson apologized to Tickle for the trouble, but the driver was more concerned that he would have been frisked and found to be carrying a bottle of whiskey in the breast pocket of his jacket. "I was a little concerned because we had to stop at one place to get him another bottle of whiskey," Jackson said. He added with a sympathetic tone, "But he drove pretty straight."

The next landmark was Brigham City, Utah. Howard Tickle was smooth sailing compared to the next cast of characters that drove him through the night all the way to Portland, Oregon.

The driver and passenger were recently released from prison in Chattanooga, Tennessee. By the sounds of it, it probably wasn't too long before they were back behind bars. The two were drinking and drugging along the way. Jackson tried to form an escape plan, but his bag, which contained his wrestling gear and all of his other possessions, was in the trunk, so he felt trapped. And Jackson was the second hitchhiker in the vehicle. The other had a bag stocked with marijuana and pills and was helping himself to his supply and offering his stock to the others as well. Jackson's only thoughts were, *How did I get myself into this mess and how do I get out of it?*

On a wing and a prayer, he made it to the outskirts of Portland, where he took a welcomed, uneventful ride to Seattle. He was dropped off near a bridge that he walked across to reach his final destination.

He arrived on the University of Washington campus on Saturday afternoon, two and a half days after being dropped off outside Manhattan. He was exhausted.

He entered Hec Edmundson Pavilion[2] and found his way to the wrestling room, where he was greeted by the University of Washington wrestling team, practicing and working out the kinks before the big event ahead of them. Jackson just wanted to find a place to rest.

Mike D'Antuono was head coach Jim Smith's assistant during the

1972-73 season. He remembers that Jackson came into the wrestling room looking for coaches. "After he introduced himself, Coach Smith and I just sort of took him under our wing from then on," he said from his Southern California home in 2024. D'Antuono helped facilitate putting him up at the Sigma Nu fraternity house.

Hec Edmundson Pavilion on the campus of the University of Washington, site of the 1973 NCAA wrestling championships. *Photo Credit: Seattle Times.*

The weary traveler spent the next thirty hours hibernating. After his slumber, he was ready to prepare for the biggest wrestling tournament of his life. The UW program stepped up again. It provided for his room and board and adopted him as part of its team, inviting him to its practice sessions. They all called him the "Kansas Flash," a name others would adopt when word began spreading beyond the UW wrestling team.

In one memorable exchange after a practice, Washington's heavyweight Dave Graves approached Jackson and asked where he was from. When Jackson said, "Ark City, Kansas," Graves told him he hailed from Blackwell, Oklahoma, just a stone's throw from Arkansas City and only a twenty-minute drive from Jackson's birthplace of Newkirk, Oklahoma.

As it turns out, the University of Washington qualified wrestlers for the 1973 nationals in nine of the ten weight classes. Jackson's weight class, 134 pounds, was the only one where the Huskies did not have an entry. Serendipity!

Coach D'Antuono recalls that the UW contingent of coaches and wrestlers took care of Jackson during his matches. He doesn't remember the exact cornering situation, but even during his matches, the Huskies took care of their adopted 134-pounder.

He also vividly remembers the Sigman Nu fraternity getting behind Jackson during the competition. "A whole group of fraternity guys came to the tournament and became his personal rooting section," he said.

The Washington program was impressed by Jackson's remarkable determination. A contact was made to a local TV news reporter who came out, then another from a competing station. A national news program contacted him. The story was picked up by the Associated Press (AP) and made available for newspapers across the nation. Support started coming in, in the form of encouraging words and financial backing.

News outlets in Manhattan, Kansas, were not exempt from receiving the information. Letters began piling up on Ernie Barrett's desk, none supporting his decision. By today's standards, Wayne Jackson had "gone viral."

Wayne Jackson's senior season photo (1973-74).
Photo Credit: Collegian Media Group.

His goal of simply wanting to compete was genuine. He did not solicit attention or funding. He turned down offers of bus and plane tickets to get him home. He donated cash that was given to him (totaling several hundred dollars) to the Washington Husky wrestling program. Over $1,000 had either been promised or handed to him. "I got there myself, I figured I should get home by myself too," is how Jackson explains his "thanks, but no thanks" attitude.

During the days leading up to the tournament, the Kansas Flash was the talk of the town. Celebrity TV sports commentator Frank Gifford met with Jackson and filmed him demonstrating scoring techniques for the Wild World of Sports broadcast that would air in the coming weeks.

Oklahoma State University coach, Tommy Chesbro, told Jackson, "You and Chris Taylor are the most famous people here." Taylor, Iowa State's 400-pound heavyweight, drew crowds wherever he went. He was fresh off a bronze medal performance at the 1972 Munich Olympics and would pin his way through the '73 NCAA tournament.

Roger Fisher (left), Chris Taylor, and Wayne Jackson pose for a picture in the newly constructed Hilton Coliseum on the campus of Iowa State University. Taylor drew crowds wherever he went. The 6' 5" 400-pound heavyweight was NCAA champion in 1972 and 1973 and won a bronze medal in the 1972 Olympics. *Photo Credit:* Wayne Jackson personal collection.

As the tournament began, attention shifted from the anomaly to the normal. It was Dan Gable's first year on the University of Iowa coaching staff as Gary Kurdelmeier's assistant.[3] Taylor would lead the Cyclones to the team title. Pinning machine Wade Schalles put tiny Clarion University on the map with an NCAA title in '72 and a repeat in '73. His unusual style accounted for falls in eight out of ten matches he wrestled during the two NCAA tournaments. Oregon State's national champion Greg Strobel led a strong contingent of West Coast wrestlers. His Beavers would finish as NCAA runner-up.

Jackson didn't have the tournament he was aiming for. His 7-3 victory over Tim Vance of Utah State in the opening round was followed by a 14-5 loss to #3 seed Laron Hansen from Brigham Young. Hansen advanced to the semifinals to send Jackson to the consolation bracket, where he met Auburn's Dave Cathey and picked up an 8-4 win to stay alive. In the next round, University of Michigan's sixth-seeded Jeff Guyton eliminated Jackson with an 11-1 victory.

It wasn't a made-for-Hollywood Cinderella story, but going 2-2 at the NCAA tournament is a respectable showing—even for athletes from programs with all the trappings needed for success. In the Big Eight and NCAA tournaments Jackson's three losses were all to eventual All-Americans.

Wayne Jackson, 1972-73 season.
Photo Credit: Collegian Media Group.

Darrell Keller and his identical twin, Dwayne, were NCAA champions for Oklahoma State who had finished their eligibility a few years prior and were helping out as assistant coaches at their alma mater. Originally from Washington, Darrell had driven out to nationals and was driving back to Stillwater after the event.

He was aware of Jackson's situation and offered to take him back with him and his group, which included Dennis Crowe (also originally from Washington and an All-American at OSU) and another passenger. It was a fun drive back and much less colorful than the trip out to Seattle!

Spring break at K-State followed the NCAA tournament, so Jackson was dropped off in Ark City en route to the group's final destination, Stillwater, just over an hour's drive south. He would have a few days to recuperate at home before returning to the K-State campus.

When Jackson returned, he was notified that Barrett had called a meeting with the wrestling team. It was not for a cake-and-punch reception or photo ops with university dignitaries. Barrett let Jackson have it in front of his peers. He was told that a "stack of letters" was on his desk and that his actions made the university look bad. Jackson reiterated to Barrett that he did not intend to harm the university. He earned the right to compete in the NCAA tournament and simply wanted to pursue his dream of earning All-American honors.

Among the letters and newspaper articles were those from the ranks of wrestling alumni. Dwight Hemmerling, a 1971 grad and NCAA qualifier, penned a letter to the editor that ran in the March 7, 1973 edition of the *Manhattan Mercury*. Dee Gard wrote a letter to Barrett and received a response from him explaining the financial strains the university was under as the reason for not funding the trip to the NCAAs.

In retrospect, Jackson's journey likely kept the program on life-support for two more seasons. Had the publicity not focused attention on the program, it may have been quietly eliminated and justified as a cost-savings measure.

Interestingly, Jackson's story and the plight of K-State wrestling parallel Shane Griffith, Stanford University, and his 2021 NCAA title, credited with saving the Cardinal wrestling program and other Olympic sports at the prestigious university. For more information, simply do an internet search to learn about this incredible story. The issues with funding wrestling programs and others labeled "non-revenue" have not gone away.

The next chapter explores the new hire, Fred Fozzard, and factors that led to K-State's wrestling program being eliminated.

Chapter Seven Endnotes: *"Going my way?"*

1. Samuelson lost in the opening round to Kit Kuntze of Princeton by a 13-9 decision in the 142-pound bracket. He did not have the opportunity to continue competing in the consolation bracket due to Kuntze's loss in the next round.
2. Hec Edmundson Pavilion, or "Hec Ed" to the locals, is still the indoor sports arena on the University of Washington campus, site of the 1973 NCAA Wrestling Championships. Now called Alaska Airlines Arena at Hec Edmundson Pavilion, it has undergone renovations and expansions and is now a modern facility with a seating capacity of 10,000.
3. Dan Gable, a 1972 Munich Olympics gold medalist and two-time NCAA champion for Iowa State, would go on to lead the Hawkeyes to fifteen NCAA titles and a 355–21–5 dual record from 1976-97 when he was head coach.

-8-
I am Woman, Hear Me Roar!

After Fritz Knorr's death, Coach Dale Samuelson was the easy choice for a temporary fix. However, during the transition, he was not labeled "interim head coach," and a national search was not announced. Going forward, Samuelson was the guy.

Times were tough in Manhattan, and spending money on a seasoned coach would be costly. The coach would likely come up with ideas for improving and expanding the program, ideas that would also come with a price tag. Keeping the status quo and making do seemed to be the approach. Jackson and his hitchhiking adventure forced the hand and likely kept the program from being dropped after the 1972-73 season.

Athletic Director Ernie Barrett began a search for the best available candidate. Like Michael Ahearn in the 1920s, Barrett looked south to Stillwater to tap into the tradition-rich Oklahoma State program.

Fred Fozzard was chosen to lead the Wildcats. He was a "name" in wrestling circles. The strapping Oklahoma State grad won the 1967 NCAA championship at 177 pounds. He also earned two additional All-American honors[1] and was a member of two NCAA champion teams in 1966 and '68 under the direction of Hall of Famer Myron Roderick[2]. When hired by K-State, Fozzard was an assistant for the Pokes on Head Coach Tommy Chesbro's staff.

Fozzard's resume from his competition days also includes a world championship at 82 kilograms (180.5 pounds). In 1969 Fozzard and fellow Oregonian Rick Sanders became the first-ever freestyle world champions for the United States when they traveled to Mar del Plata, Argentina, along with a strong contingent of American wrestlers.[3]

Fozzard also made the 1970 U.S. Freestyle World Team at 82 KG. He finished in 5th place in Edmonton, Canada.

Fred Fozzard, three-time All-American and NCAA champion at Oklahoma State. *Photo Credit*: Oklahoma State University Archives.

Fozzard (top row, third from right) was a member of the star-studded 1966 NCAA championship team for Oklahoma State. Wellington, Kansas native Myron Roderick was head coach, pictured in the top row, far right. *Photo Credit*: Oklahoma State University Archives.

Fozzard seemed to be just what was needed to elevate the Wildcats to a place at the table with Big Eight and NCAA perennial powers Oklahoma State, Oklahoma, and Iowa State. The hire was ushered in with hope and promise within the Kansas wrestling community. Barrett couldn't have made a better hire.

Fozzard (top row, far right) was an assistant during Tommy Chesbro's first year as head coach at Oklahoma State, 1969-70. He remained in that position for four years until taking on the head coaching role at Kansas State.
Photo Credit: Oklahoma State University Archives.

Part of the initial excitement was stoked with a fundraising tour that introduced the new coach to the Wildcat faithful. In July of 1973, Barrett and Fozzard appeared in Garden City, Hays, Norton, St. Francis, Colby, Atwood, and ten other western Kansas towns that were known to prioritize the sport of wrestling in their communities. Barrett sang the new coach's praises, and Fozzard laid out plans to bring wrestling to competitive levels that were on par with the elite programs. During the tour, Barrett noted that K-State wrestling's annual budget of $40,000 was not competitive with Iowa State, Oklahoma, or Oklahoma State, which all spent around $100,000 annually on the sport. An organized fundraising campaign was communicated, and each county was challenged to meet the goal of $1,600 to match the cost of a full scholarship.

After the initial splash, however, the positive outlook didn't take long to turn. Fozzard's time in Manhattan was marked by conflict with the administration almost from the start and financial problems within the wrestling program and the entire athletic department.

Newspaper accounts show that Fozzard was trying to modernize the program with new mats and a score clock, but funding even those basic items was a struggle. He also publicized the desire to host camps for wrestlers, clinics for coaches, and tournaments to attract the wrestling community to campus and help offset the costs of running a college wrestling program. His enthusiasm for these endeavors was not shared with the administration. Approval for scheduling and venue use was met with delays and a lack of shared vision.

Fozzard, who will turn 80 in June of 2025, lives in the central Oregon community of La Pine. He has long since left behind any ill feelings toward his time in Manhattan. "That was a long time ago. I was young and the school was struggling financially. I don't blame anyone for what happened," he said.

Today, Fozzard focuses on painting and looking after his roommate, Doug Campbell, a two-time National Qualifier at OSU when Fozzard began his coaching career there in the early 1970s. These days, he is less mobile and unable to venture out much. "I paint with acrylics on canvas. I mostly paint owls and other birds, deer, and scenes from the area. Central Oregon is a beautiful part of the country," he said.

Once an elite competitor and high-level coach, Fozzard has withdrawn from the wrestling world. The 2012 National Wrestling Hall of Fame Distinguished Member inductee doesn't display awards or memorabilia from his glory days and does not follow current events and results from the sport. "That was in the past. I have pretty well moved on from that," he said. "I'm not even sure where most of my trophies and medals are anymore," he added.

Fozzard does not recall a particular incident that was the tipping point, but he began to get the impression early on that wrestling was not a priority at K-State and his efforts to build the program were not appreciated. "It seems that instead of helping me, they [administration] resisted my ideas, and it was hard to get approval for any expenditures at all," he recalls.

Fozzard was the head coach for only two seasons. He was fired on April 25, 1975, after Barrett gave him the option of resigning on his own or being dismissed. Nearly fifty years later, the way Fozzard remembers why he chose the latter option is because he didn't want to let the kids down. "I wanted to show them that I stood by them and fought for them to the last," he said.

There seems to be no evidence that an interim coach was appointed or that a search for a new coach was initiated after Fozzard's firing. The wrestling program, golf, and tennis were officially dropped on July 24, 1975, three months after Fozzard was dismissed.

John Stroble has a unique perspective on the final season of K-State wrestling. The 1974 state champion at 167 pounds for Newton High helped his school win the Kansas 4A team title under the direction of Hall of Fame coach Delbert Erickson. He caught the eye of Coach Fozzard and was part of the last recruiting class of Kansas State wrestling.

With an injury to starter John Kadel, the true freshman was thrust into the lineup. He speaks highly of his time at K-State and Coach Fozzard. "I had a wonderful experience up there. I can't say anything bad about my experience. And evidently Fred had a whole lot to do with that because he hid all of the stuff that was negative. I'm going to have to find a way to tell him how much I appreciate it because I had a wonderful experience because of it. That is pure unselfishness and shows a whole lot of character on his part," said Stroble from his home in Oklahoma in 2024.

It sounds almost implausible through a modern lens, but Stroble was unaware that Fozzard had been fired and the program axed until he returned to campus for a camp in July that had been scheduled for months. After the season ended in March, there were no organized practices, as is the case in most college programs today. Stroble kept to himself and didn't have much contact with the program during that off-season. The spring semester ended, and he returned to Newton for his summer job and a break from college life.

When Fozzard contacted him about returning to campus to help work the wrestling camp, he jumped at the opportunity to help out and get in some training before the fall semester. What he wasn't expecting was that Fozzard's real motivation for inviting him to the camp was to introduce him to suitors for a possible transfer so that he could continue his wrestling career.

Fozzard made arrangements with several college coaching colleagues to attend the camp. Stroble again praises Fozzard for the gesture. "He didn't have to do that, but he was looking out for me and other teammates and wanted the best for us," he said.

Stroble landed at Central State University in Edmond, Oklahoma. The school, now known as the University of Central Oklahoma, was then a wrestling power in the NAIA ranks and is now a wrestling power in NCAA DII after its 1989 transition. The Broncos wrapped up their seventeenth national title in program history in March 2024 when the nationals were held at Hartman Arena in Park City, Kansas. The program now has eight NCAA DII titles to complement the nine from its time in NAIA.

Stroble was a force in the Broncos' lineup. During his senior season, he earned All-American honors by finishing fifth at 177 pounds at the 1978 NAIA nationals.

There were others who transferred out to continue competing and others who decided to give up the sport. Bruce Randall was a K-State freshman in the fall of 1973, Fozzard's first recruiting class.

The Perry, Oklahoma native joined his older brother, Steve, at Oklahoma State when the K-State program was dropped to finish out his career on the mat and in the classroom.

Sophomore Bruce Randall, the last NCAA Qualifier in K-State history. He was in the same bracket as his brother, Steve, who finished in fourth place for Oklahoma State at 142 pounds at the 1975 NCAAs. Bruce transferred to OSU and finished out his eligibility. *Photo Credit*: Collegiate Media Group.

Perry is only a thirty-minute drive to OSU's Stillwater campus, which, coupled with his brother being part of the program, made the transfer a no-brainer. He didn't even consider other options but would have liked to finish his career at Kansas State. "I wish I could have completed my career at K-State to see what I could have done," he said. In Manhattan, he was an important cog in the starting lineup. In Stillwater, he was stuck behind Steve Barrett and Lee Roy Smith, who both became NCAA champions.[4]

Steve is two years older than Bruce. When he came to campus to observe practice sessions as a high schooler, Fozzard made an impression on him. "Fred was always friendly to me when I was around visiting my brother. Chesbro [OSU's head coach] didn't acknowledge me like Fozzard did," he said. When choosing a college, Randall was excited about becoming a Wildcat and competing under Fozzard's leadership. It also didn't hurt that K-State offered a full-ride scholarship and OSU only a partial.

Randall has the distinction of being the final NCAA tournament participant in Kansas State University Wrestling history by qualifying for the 1975 NCAA tournament at 142 pounds. He was K-State's lone qualifier that season.

He also has another rare distinction that went along with being part of the 142-pound bracket. His brother, Steve, represented Oklahoma State and was the top seed—in the same weight class! Bruce went 0-2, and Steve wound up in fourth place. The two didn't meet in the tournament but did end up in the same half of the consolation bracket and would have met in the blood round, or match to earn All-American status, if Bruce had made it that far.

The first known brothers to compete in the same weight class are the Deppe Brothers, Tom (Lehigh) and Daniel (Michigan) at 123 pounds at the 1955 NCAA Championships. Daniel finished in fourth-place, Tom went 0-1. since then, it has happened a handful of times, but is a rare occurrence.[5]

Bruce, who now lives in Arkansas, reflects on his move to OSU and finishing his career there. "The biggest difference was the competition in the room being so much deeper at OSU," he said. He also noted that Fozzard's techniques and style were unorthodox compared to the more basic and structured instruction that was part of Tommy Chesbro's methods. He remembers both programs running physically demanding practices.

As a young college student, Randall doesn't recall being very aware of the financial strains that the athletic department was going through. He was there to go to school and wrestle, and Fozzard didn't draw the team into the drama that was taking place behind the scenes.

Randall does point to his feelings that Title IX and the football team's poor showing contributed to the financial problems. "I just wanted to wrestle, so I didn't involve myself in that part. With Title IX and the football program being so poor, there wasn't much money to go around," he said. He wishes the university would have treated the wrestlers better on their way out. "They didn't even let us keep our gear. They made us turn it in. I mean, what were they going to do with it, the program was being dropped," he questioned.

Fozzard seemed to be the right coach, but times were tough, and the K-State wrestling program was caught in layers of circumstances that each contributed to an impossible situation that was doomed to failure.

Ernie Barrett himself did not escape the turmoil. On Tuesday, December 16, 1975, Mr. K-State was relieved of his duties. President Duane Acker (newly hired on July 1, 1975) softened the blow by announcing that Barrett would be assigned to, "another important position to be announced later."[6] After accepting the demotion, Barrett announced days later that effective January 31, 1976, he would resign from his new position as Assistant to the President for Special Projects.

Ernie Barrett served as athletic director during the most trying time in the history of K-State athletics. *Photo Credit: Manhattan Mercury.*

An interesting side note in the K-State Athletic Director movement is the connection to one of the greatest coaches and dynasties in NCAA history, Dan Gable, and the Iowa Hawkeyes.

Barrett's replacement was John "Jersey" Jermier, who was coming from an assistant athletic director role at the University of Iowa. When he left for Manhattan, Iowa's head wrestling coach, Gary Kurdelmeier, assumed Jermier's vacated position, which left Gable to fill the void left by Kurdelmeier. Most expected the twenty-seven-year-old assistant to take over for Kurdelmeier, but when Jermier left, things likely fell into place on an accelerated timeline.

"It was ironic that this all happened at a time when Iowa State University was showing interest in me and looking for me to come back," Gable recalls in a 2024 interview. The Cyclones weren't content with the Hawkeyes gaining the upper hand in the state and nationally. Even head coach Harold Nichols was interested in bringing his prize pupil back to Ames to take his job. "I was not promised the head position at Iowa, so I was willing to listen," he said.

The 1970 Big 8 championships were held at Ahearn Coliseum, where Dan Gable of Iowa State won his third conference title. Two weeks later, Gable would lose his only match during high school and college when Washington's Larry Owings defeated him at the NCAA championship at Northwestern University. Gable would go on to Olympic Gold in 1972 and an unparalleled coaching career at the University of Iowa. *Photo Credit*: Collegiate Media Group.

The K-State opening seems to have happened at the right time for the Iowa faithful. "Kurdelmeier told me about Jersey leaving and that he was moving into his position. I thought I had a good chance to get the job," he said. Fifteen NCAA titles and twenty-one consecutive Big Ten titles are strong evidence that athletic director C. W. "Bump" Elliott made the right hire.

"I had a good relationship with Jersey Jermier and was very close to him. He was supportive and wanted the best for the wrestling program at Iowa. I was hoping he would be able to reinstate wrestling at Kansas State, but with the economics and other issues, that didn't happen," Gable said.

Kansas State's Lyle Cook (far right) finished in fourth place in the 142-pound bracket at the 1970 Big 8 tournament. He lost by fall to Gable (far left) in the semifinals. *Photo Credit:* Collegiate Media Group.

Nichols remained head coach at Iowa State until 1985, when Jim Gibbons took over.

Barrett returned to K-State in the late 1980s when Athletic Director Steve Miller invited him back as a fundraising consultant. By 1991, he had become the athletic department's director of development. He retired from that post in 2007 when he was seventy-eight years old. During his time away from K-State, starting in the mid-70s, he worked for Davis Paint Company in Kansas City, Missouri, and later for Chief Drilling Company in Wichita.

Communication and personnel issues aside, weathering the financial storm was an uphill battle. Fozzard sold advertisements on schedule posters with the hopes of raising enough money to produce a film with the working title of "The Kansas Wrestler" to promote the program and increase the size of the fan base. He also worked to add cheerleaders to draw in bigger crowds to home duals. Hosting kids' tournaments and inviting youth clubs to compete against each other as part of home duals was another creative way of increasing attendance.

Fozzard hustled to gain more notoriety and earn money for the program. These efforts might have paid off in more stable financial times, but they amounted to only a light mist when a gully washer was needed.

Fozzard was still young and only a few years removed from a gold medal at the 1969 World Championships. He considered entering the 1976 Olympic Trials in an attempt to represent Team USA at the Montreal Olympics. He figured it would attract recruits, bring publicity to the university and its wrestling program, and provide a possible financial shot in the arm through sponsorship. When he informed Barrett of his intentions, he was surprised at his boss's lack of support. "He felt that it showed a lack of commitment to the program due to the time I would have to train and be away," said Fozzard.

1974-75 was the final season in Kansas State University wrestling history. World Champion and former Oklahoma State assistant coach, Fred Fozzard, was the last coach. *Photo Credit*: Oklahoma State University Archives.

The tennis program, which was eventually dropped along with wrestling and golf, was also in financial straits. In a creative fundraising effort, the program sponsored a concert featuring the world-renowned band Kansas, which netted a healthy profit.

The athletic council thought it would be a good idea to sponsor a copycat event to benefit the entire athletic program. Hellen Reddy was booked for a concert on Friday, February 7, 1975.

What seemed like a good idea was a snub to the wrestling program. A home dual with Central Missouri State University, scheduled months before the Hellen Reddy concert was even a thought, had to be moved to the Mule's campus in Warrensburg.

The concert was poorly promoted and poorly attended. The flop not only failed to raise the expected revenue but also caused Olivia Newton-John to cancel. She was negotiating with K-State, but Newton-John was tired of waiting and booked a show elsewhere due to the scrutiny of the failed Reddy concert.

Helen Reddy performed a benefit concert for the KSU Athletic Department in February 1973. A home wrestling dual had to be moved to the guest's arena to accommodate the concert. The event fell short of its fundraising goals and came to symbolize the struggles that led to the end of K-State wrestling.
Photo Credit: Collegiate Media Group.

"I am woman, hear me roar!"[7]

Football's impact on the entire athletic budget caused bigger financial woes. Football, then and now, is the economic driver at major universities. The health of all athletic programs is tied closely to what football brings in through gate receipts, advertising dollars, and donations.

Today, Wildcat football is one of the top draws in the entire state. Bill Snyder's "Miracle in Manhattan" brought the program from its ashes, starting after his hiring in 1988.

The capacity of The Bill[8] is 50,000, and empty seats for home football games are rare today. In 1974, by comparison, average home game attendance was down to 9,000. The program was a laughingstock of the Big Eight. On top of everything else, a football team on a losing streak could not feed a hungry family of seventeen sports.[9]

Notably, in January 1975, Ellis Rainsberger was hired as head football coach to replace Vince Gibson. Rainsberger understood his task of winning and filling stadium seats. He also appreciated the role of football in the total health of K-State athletics. Originally from East St. Louis, Illinois, he was a standout football player for the Wildcats and a member of the wrestling team from 1954-57.

The ill-fated Rainsberger era lasted three seasons, from 1975-77. The Cats went 6-27 during that span without a single Big Eight win. It wasn't a downturn that anyone can blame on Rainsberger. In the twenty-five seasons from 1957-81, K-State had only one winning season, a 6-5 record in 1970.

Before leaving football's impact, it has to be mentioned that Oklahoma University football also impacted the bottom line of the K-State athletic department. OU football? Yes, you read that correctly. Among other penalties, OU was placed on a bowl ban for 1973 and 1974 due to NCAA violations. With the ban went the Big Eight Conference's share of bowl and television money, doled out to member schools. K-State relied on its big brother to come through in the national rankings to gather a fat check for being selected to play in a marquee bowl game.

Barrett made it clear that football and basketball would continue to be funded at adequate levels, even at the expense of other programs. And who could blame him? If not for those programs, the ship would sink. Basketball, and especially football, was the ship, with the passengers being the vulnerable non-revenue programs. Times were desperate and tough decisions had to be made.

To show just how desperate the situation was, a proposal was brought forth to eliminate scholarships for all minor sports in an attempt to avoid dropping programs. For clarification, "minor sports" is not meant to be slight. That was how sports other than football and basketball were termed at the time. Today you may see the term "Olympic" or "non-revenue" sports to describe that category.

On December 3, 1974, the athletic council announced that scholarships for all minor sports would be phased out over the next three years. Part of that headline was the first domino to fall: men's gymnastics, which was already operating without scholarships, would be eliminated at the conclusion of the 1974-75 school year. The outcry among coaches and supporters was loud and strong, forcing the athletic council to shelf the proposal and go back to the drawing board to find cost-saving measures.

On Valentine's Day 1975, the Kansas State wrestling program hosted its final event of the season—and ever. Central State University, ranked #1 in the nation in NAIA, came to town to complete a home and away series. The Broncos took a 24-20 victory at home in December and made it a sweep with a 25-15 win at Ahearn.

The Cats finished the season with a 5-11 dual mark and a sixth place showing in the Big Eight tournament, finishing ahead of only the Colorado Buffaloes with five points and a single national qualifier.

The NCAA tournament, held at Princeton University in New Jersey from March 13-15, 1975, would be K-State's last wrestling competition. Forty-one days later, Fozzard was dismissed, and three months later, the door was slammed shut on the program for good.

Yes, times were tough within K-State athletics, but they weren't much better anywhere across the U.S.

In 1973, the Organization of the Petroleum Exporting Countries (OPEC) brought on an oil embargo. Gas prices soared, and consumers endured long lines at gas stations. The economy was in a recession from November 1973 to March 1975. In 1973, inflation doubled to 8.8 percent and remained high through the early 1980s. Unemployment hovered around eight percent in the years surrounding the end of the K-State wrestling program.

For families trying to keep gas in their cars and food on the table, there were bigger concerns than funding drowning sports programs at their favorite university.

Some incorrectly point to Title IX as the preeminent reason for K-State wrestling's demise. The legislation passed on June 23, 1972, to end sex-based discrimination in educational institutions was still being sorted out during K-State wrestling's decline.

It was certainly a factor, but alone and in another era, it likely could have been handled without impacting existing programs.

President Duane Acker favored a consolidated athletic department housing men's and women's athletics. Ernie Barrett argued that trying to fund newly developed women's athletic programs with the existing athletic department funding structure was unfair and impractical. He felt that a standalone women's athletic department should be developed. Funding was already a strain, and taking on more was difficult to fathom.

Leo Kocher of the University of Chicago retired after the 2023-24 season. He spent forty-five years as the Maroons' head wrestling coach. The 2024 NCAA DIII Coach of the Year has been sought out over the years as an expert on issues related to Title IX; its impacts, and misapplications. He has written and presented extensively on the topic and has made TV appearances on ABC's *20/20* and *60 Minutes* (CBS), among many other news segments.

Kocher believes Title IX became part of the justification for those holding the purse strings of college wrestling programs to discontinue rather than add sports to balance gender equity. It is a cruel irony that the legislation was passed during economic hardship for the country and at K-State, where other factors exacerbated the wrestling program's demise.

"The way the law was essentially interpreted was equal numbers of males and females. Intentionally or not, its design gave athletic administrators cover for dropping programs. The hammer was the ability of the government to withhold federal funds if institutions did not reach proportionality," he said.

The Three Prongs of Proportionality, Expansion, and Accommodating Interests that are often cited today, did not come into effect until years after wrestling was dropped at K-State. "During the initial phases of interpretation after the legislation was passed, there was little guidance but great concern of non-compliance penalties. It was a bit of the case of building the plane as it was being flown. As it applied to athletics,[10] many institutions cut sports or limited roster numbers for male sports because not being proportional really wasn't an option," said Kocher.

This was concerning for all sports because there weren't women participants to help balance the numbers at the time. For K-State, it was another justification to drop wrestling. "On top of everything else at places like Kansas State, with federal funding at stake, it was the easy thing to do," said Kocher. He added, "And let's face it, to most universities' central administration the most important quality of an athletic director is to do what he/she is told to do, rather than doing the educationally sound, ethical thing, which puts their federal funding at risk."

The fall of the K-State wrestling program is a study of the signs of the times. Economic conditions, program management in the face of how to best implement Title IX requirements, and interpersonal relationships formed a toxic mix that was simply too much to bear.

Take a walk through the athletic facilities at Kansas State University today. They are impressive. Bill Snyder Family Stadium and surrounding training facilities rival any major college football complex. Bramlage Coliseum, now connected to "The Bill," has a seating capacity of 12,500 and the look and feel of an elite basketball arena.

The Morris Family Olympic Training Center, completed in 2023, is connected to the Morgan Family Arena, a 3,100-seat arena where the volleyball team plays. The other sports also have first-class training and competition facilities that match the luster of football, basketball, and volleyball.

Could wrestling fit into the mix of sports at K-State? Men's and women's programs? Don't hold your breath. The price tag for a start-up would be daunting. A four or five-mat facility with a weight room, locker room, and lounge would be required. Volleyball or track and field likely aren't interested in giving up real estate in their facilities to make room for a wrestling program. An addition to a current building or a stand-alone facility would need to be constructed at a cost well into the double-digit millions.

The start-up costs are one thing, the ongoing costs are another. After submitting Freedom of Information Act (FOIA) requests to obtain the budgets of comparable institutions, the following numbers were gathered from Iowa State University and Oklahoma State University.

In 2022-23, the Cowboys spent $2.3 million on their wrestling program, with $1.3 million to cover personnel, $500,000 for scholarships, and another $500,000 for operational costs. The Cyclones spent a similar amount: $2.4 million. About $550,000 went to operational expenses, the rest to scholarships and personnel. Iowa State's data also included income. The program brought in just over $330,000.

Neither ISU nor OSU currently supports a varsity women's wrestling program; few do at the NCAA DI level.[11] The University of Iowa is currently the only major DI school to support a women's wrestling program. That will certainly change in the coming years as women's wrestling moves from emerging sports status to championship status.[12]

According to information obtained through a FOIA request from the University of Iowa, Kansas State University would have to be prepared for mammoth-sized numbers if it is considering starting and sustaining both men's and women's wrestling programs.

University of Iowa head men's coach, Tom Brands and Company oversaw total operating expenses of $3,577,937 in 2022-23 and total operating revenues of $2,311,769 for its program of thirty-eight wrestlers.

Clarissa Chun and her Iowa women's wrestling staff had total operating expenses of $846,991 and total operating revenues of

$418,141 during the 2022-23 school year for their roster of sixteen. These figures reflect the program's start-up year. The 2023-24 season was the first with a competition schedule. The program now has a full staff and roster of twenty-six athletes.

In addition to the university expenditures for a wrestling program, a competitive DI wrestling program would have to host a regional training center (RTC).

Regional training centers were approved by the NCAA in 2009 to serve athletes training in the international styles of freestyle and Greco-Roman during the off-season and as post-grads. USA Wrestling is charged with approving sites and compliance, which includes setting criteria for eligibility to train at an established RTC and guidelines for all involved to stay in good standing with USA Wrestling. RTCs have their own budgets, separate from the money needed to operate the college program. Attracting the best resident athletes and coaches is a significant financial ask of donors, but it is necessary to stay competitive with the top programs.

Aside from facility and budget concerns and assisting with developing a robust RTC, a program like K-State would also have to concern itself with "name, image, and likeness" (NIL) implications, which have also been added to the plate of college athletics. Today, top athletes expect to make personal financial gains while representing their school, and athletic departments are expected to help them navigate through the dos and don'ts.

Yet another wrinkle in modern big-time college athletic programs is the NCAA transfer portal. If athletes see the need, they may hit the portal and take their talents elsewhere, another reason for colleges to offer the best coaching, facilities, and connections.

It is becoming impractical for universities to make room for additional programs at the DI level when sustaining what they already have is stretching resources to the limit.

At the same time, wrestling is at a unique place in its history in the United States. It enjoys unprecedented success on the international stage at all age levels, and its popularity at the scholastic level is strong.

Wrestling is among the fastest-growing sports for high school and collegiate females. Rather than list the forty-seven states that have sanctioned wrestling at the high school level, it is now easier to mention Vermont and Delaware as the only states left to fully sanction. In Virginia, girls' wrestling has emerging sports status.

In the 2025-26 school year, the NCAA is scheduled to sanction women's wrestling as a championship sport. 2024 marked the second year of a sanctioned women's national tournament in the NAIA, and the NJCAA is on track to sanction a tournament for its junior college programs in the coming years.

The most recent boys' participation numbers put wrestling at #6, behind soccer and ahead of cross country in U.S. high schools. The number of men's college programs has bounced back from years of decline, with enrollment-driven private schools leading the way.

The sport of wrestling is thriving at the high school level, but what factors make it more difficult to add at the major-college level of the NCAA?

Kansas State University Athletic Director, Gene Taylor, has been at K-State since 2017. He had prior stops at wrestling-rich universities when he was deputy athletics director at the University of Iowa from 2014-17 and athletic director at North Dakota State University from 2001-14.

Taylor would like to see athletic opportunities expand at K-State but understands that it is not practical in today's environment. "Do you want just to have a program, or do you want it to be competitive on the same level as programs like Iowa State, Oklahoma State, and Oklahoma? We would want to be competitive, and it just doesn't make sense right now with what we are facing in college athletics," he said.

Aside from the start-up costs and finding the right coach, Taylor also points to NIL, revenue sharing, and long-term funding commitments as barriers. "Things have changed from even a few years ago making it very difficult to consider," he said. "Wrestling is a sport that I've always loved. I just don't think it is something that we could reasonably consider at this time," he said. He added that wrestling on the men's side and softball on the women's side are the two sports that the K-State athletic department gets the most inquiries about adding.

During the first eight months of 2024, the wrestling community witnessed Penn State's record-breaking NCAA tournament performance, John Smith's retirement, the Olympic Trials, Oklahoma State's dramatic hiring of David Taylor, and Team USA's performance at the Paris Olympics, where the men's freestyle team failed to win gold for the first time since 1968 but did add three medals to its historical total.[13] The women's team that had a record finish by collecting four medals, including golds from Sarah Hildebrandt (50 KG) and twenty-year-old Amit Elor (68 KG).[14]

During that same time period, Lindenwood University in St. Charles, Missouri, completed the final season of its men's wrestling program after beginning the transition to NCAA DI in February of 2022.

After thirty-four years,[15] which included a solid run in the NCAA DII ranks and five NAIA national titles,[16] the program is no more. Preserving Lindenwood's stats and stories must be a priority, or they will be forever lost. Time moves on. If not recorded and archived, future generations will miss out on the history that was a significant part of the lives of sons, fathers, grandfathers, families, and supporters.

A solution has not been found. As this manuscript goes to press, Cleveland State University announced that the 2024-25 season would be its last. Its history dates back to 1931 when it was known as Fenn College, and the program has been in continuous operation since 1962.

Earlier in the 2024-25 season, Campbell University in Buies Creek, North Carolina, announced a plan to drastically scale back support of its Olympic sports on campus. The wrestling program, founded in 1968, has been a model of a mid-major doing things right off the mat and getting results on it.

America itself needs more, not less wrestling programs to test young people and give them the ability to persevere through setbacks by hard work and dedication to a cause. If the current funding model continues to move forward, it likely won't be long before other similarly positioned programs will be counted among wrestling's casualties. If that happens, those histories, like those at Lindenwood,

Campbell, and Cleveland State, must be preserved. I hope *K-State's Wrestling Legacy* will keep the Kansas State wrestling light flickering for future generations to appreciate.

Chapter Eight Endnotes: *I am Woman, Hear Me Roar*

1. Fozzard was NCAA runner-up in 1966 and finished in third place as a senior in 1969, both at 177 pounds.
2. Roderick, coincidentally, is a Kansan hailing from Winfield.
3. Team USA finished behind only the Soviets in the team standings at the 1969 World Championships with golds from Sanders (52 KG) and Fozzard (82 KG), sliver from Don Behm (57 KG), Wayne Wells (74 KG), and Larry Kristoff (100 KG), and a bronze Medal from Henry Schenk (90 KG).
4. Steve Barrett was NCAA champion in 1977 at 142 pounds. Smith, of the famous wrestling family that includes former OSU head coach John Smith, won the 142-pound title in 1980.
5. In 2024, Pennsylvania brothers Luke Stout (Princeton) and younger brother Mac (Pittsburgh), both qualified for the NCAAs at 197 pounds. In 2025, the Stout brothers met in the round of 16 at the NCAA championships with Mac winning by a 4-2 score. This was the first-ever meeting between brothers at the NCAA DI tournament. In 2013, Colorado brothers Micah Burak (senior at Penn) and Nathan (freshman at Iowa) both qualified for the NCAAs at 197 pounds. In 2025, the Stout brothers met in the round of 16 at the NCAA championships with Mac winning by a 4-2 score. This was the first-ever meeting between brothers at the NCAA DI tournament. In 2010 Michigan brothers Eric Simaz (Central Michigan senior) and Cam (Cornell sophomore) were in the same bracket at 197 pounds. In 2023 at the NCAA DIII tournament, Pennsylvania brothers Nathan Lackman (senior at Rhode Island College) met his brother Matthew (a junior at Alvernia) in the finals at 165 pounds to become the first brothers to face each other in an NCAA wrestling final in any division. In 2022, Justin Portillo (Grand View) and twin brother Josh (Nebraska-Kearney) wrestled in a dual between the defending NAIA team champions and the NCAA DII champs. The dual came down to their match. Justin's overtime win gave Grandview the 22-15 victory.
6. *Salina Journal*, 12/17/75.
7. "I Am Woman" by Helen Reddy and Ray Burton, copyright Irving Music, Inc. o/b/o Buggerlugs Music Co. and Irving Music, Inc. Easy Song ID 1710733.
8. Nickname for Bill Snyder Family Stadium, where Kansas State University plays its home games.
9. During the 1974-75 school year K-State supported the following nine sports for men: baseball, basketball, cross country, football, golf, gymnastics, tennis, track & field, and wrestling along with the following eight sports for women: basketball, cross country, gymnastics, softball, swimming, tennis, track and field, and volleyball. The current list of twelve total sports include: baseball, basketball, cross country, football, golf, and track and field for men and basketball, cross country, golf, rowing, soccer, tennis, track & field, and volleyball for women.
10. It is important to know that Title IX was not an "athletics' law," but a legislation to guide all educational programming.
11. As of March 2024, according to the National Wrestling Coaches Association (NWCA), four NCAA DI programs support women's wrestling programs.

That group includes: The University of Iowa, Lindenwood University, Presbyterian College, and Sacred Heart University. Twenty-nine NCAA DII schools offer women's wrestling and sixty-two offer it at the NCAA DIII level.

12. According to the NCAA, women's wrestling, which became an emerging sport in 2020 by supporting forty programs, eclipsed that number in the 2022-23 academic year. Championship status is projected for winter 2026.

13. Spencer Lee (57 KG) won silver and Kyle Dake (74 KG) and Aaron Brooks (86 KG) both won bronze. The Greco-Roman team failed to win a match.

14. In addition to Hildebrandt and Elor, Helen Maroulis (57 KG) won bronze, and Kennedy Blades (76 KG) won silver.

15. Lindenwood had a men's wrestling program continuously for thirty-three years, from the 1990-91 school year through the 2023-24 school year. They did also support a men's program for a single season, during the 1982-83 school year.

16. 2002, 2005, 2007, 2008, 2009

Appendix A: K-State Wrestling Coaches 1922 - 1975

Edwin Arthur (E.A.) Knoth
Head Coach 1922-23 and 1924-26
(three seasons)

Born: August 28, 1897 - Cleveland, Ohio
Died: March 12, 1976 - Brevard, North Carolina
Alma Mater: Normal College of Physical Education of
Indianapolis (now part of Indiana University)

Edwin Knoth was more inclined to his academic pursuits in the physical education department at K-State, but it was also clear that he was vested in getting its wrestling program off the ground. His efforts (along with Athletic Director Michael Ahearn) eventually paid off with the hire of Buel Patterson in 1927. The Wildcats entered the fledgling Missouri Valley Conference during the 1924-25 school year while Knoth was at the helm.

Knoth gets credit for coaching the 1925-26 team, but he left in December 1925 and did not finish the season. He served as head basketball coach for the Wildcats during the 1920-21 season and was also the first boxing coach at K-State when that sport ushered in its initial season as a non-varsity sport in 1923-24.

Season	Dual Record	Missouri Valley Conference finish
1922-23	0-1	Unaffiliated with a conference
1924-25	0-0	7th place (champion: Oklahoma A&M)
1925-26	0-2-1	4th place (champion: Oklahoma A&M)

Joe Greer

Head Coach 1923-24
(one season)

Born: February 6, 1896 - Pitcairn, Pennsylvania
Died: January 9, 1955 - Dublin, Virginia
Alma Mater: Kansas State University (1925 College of
Veterinary Medicine graduate)

Joe Greer came to K-State from another agriculture school, Iowa State University, where he competed on the football, baseball, and wrestling teams. It appears that he came to Manhattan not only to coach but also to complete his veterinarian studies as part of a "federal aid vocational program."

Information is scanty on his short tenure. About all that is clear is that a team was organized, practice was held under his direction, and no competitions were held due to ineligibility and injury.

Greer played baseball at K-State during the 1925 season and served as the freshman baseball coach. He also played semi-professional baseball from 1925-28. Dr. Greer owned and operated a veterinary hospital in Virginia from 1936 until he died in 1955.

Season	Dual Record	Conference finish
1923-24	0-0	unaffiliated with a conference

O.E. Oliver Walgren
Head Coach 1925-26
(one season)

Born: June 1, 1900 - Denver, Colorado
Died: May 4, 1991 - Columbus, Nebraska
Alma Mater: Kansas State University (1926 College of
Veterinary Medicine graduate)

Oliver "Shorty" Walgren is an interesting inclusion in the coaching history of K-State wrestling. He was a student-athlete from 1923-26, but as team captain, he was charged with coaching duties during the 1925-26 season when E.A. Knoth left before the second semester.

It appeared that Frank Root, the coach of record, was little more than a supervisor, and Walgren was tasked with running practice and coaching during competitions. Walgren was also captain of the K-State boxing team. He became a veterinarian and practiced in Nebraska.

Season	Dual Record	Missouri Valley Conference finish
1925-26	0-2-1	4th place (champion: Oklahoma A&M)

Frank Root
Head Coach 1925-26
(one season)

Born: March 16, 1893 - Iola, Kansas
Died: October 15, 1959 - Lawrence, Kansas
Alma Mater: Kansas State University, 1914

Root, like Walgren, is an interesting inclusion in the head coach log. He was on the football coaching staff and filled in when E.A. Knoth left before the start of the second semester during the 1925-26 season. His role was handling administrative duties, transporting the team, and providing quotes for newspaper articles.

Root did not list "wrestling coach" on his university data sheet, dated September 1938. The document was used for media/publicity. He did list assistant football coach and basketball coach. Root served as head basketball coach at K-State from 1933-39.

Season	Dual Record	Missouri Valley Conference finish
1925-26	0-2-1	4th place (champion: Oklahoma A&M)

Gerald Northrip
Head Coach 1926-27
(one season)

Born: March 22, 1903 - Foss, Oklahoma
Died: April 6, 1984 - Richardson, Texas
Alma Mater: Oklahoma A&M, 1926

Hopes were high with the hire of Northrip, a star at Oklahoma A&M and 1925-26 Cowboy team captain. He won the 1926 National Collegiate Championship at 147 pounds when it was hosted at Oregon State University in Corvallis during the pre-NCAA era.

His coaching debut, however, was a bust, and like one-and-done Greer, not much is known about the 1926-27 season and its skipper. After one year in Manhattan, Northrip relocated to Oklahoma. It is interesting to note that according to the 1927 *Royal Purple*, "Inter-Collegiate wrestling was taken up on an extensive scale for the first time during 1926-27." Northrip was also the boxing coach during his year at K-State.

Season	Dual Record	Missouri Valley Conference finish
1926-27	0-10	4th place (champion: Oklahoma A&M)

Buel "Pat" Patterson
Head Coach 1927-47
(20 seasons)

Born: May 15, 1904 - Maynard, Arkansas (Randolph County)
Died: November 1, 1983 - Chickasha, Oklahoma
Alma Mater: Oklahoma A&M, 1934 (Bachelor of Science in Dairy Production)

After two unsuccessful attempts at harvesting top wrestlers from top programs to lead the Wildcats, Athletic Director Michael Ahearn again tapped into the treasure trove of knowledge and talent in Stillwater, but this time pulled out a plum in the next coach, Buel "Pat" Patterson.

With Pat's hire, K-State put itself on the level with the elite programs in college wrestling. He had an impressive pedigree as a national champion and team captain at Oklahoma A&M under Ed Gallagher. Also, he had a personality that drew athletes in, a calm demeanor like Gallagher, and a dogged work ethic to get things done.

Patterson not only put K-State wrestling on the map but also served as a catalyst to bring high school wrestling in the state of Kansas closer to the level of his Oklahoma roots. He was a nationally known figure in wrestling circles, serving as Chairman of the NCAA Rules Committee and administrator for the 1948 and 1952 Olympic wrestling teams. Pat went on to coach at the University of Nebraska and the University of Illinois.

At twenty seasons, Patterson was the longest-tenured coach in K-State wrestling history. He was also the boxing coach during the only two seasons that it was a varsity sport at K-State, 1935 and 1936.

Season	Dual Record	Big 6 Conference finish	NCAA top-10 finish
1927-28	2-5	7th place (the final Missouri Valley Conference tournament)	
1928-29	4-4	CHAMPION (tie with Oklahoma)	
1929-30	2-4	3rd place (champion: Oklahoma)	5th place
1930-31	5-2	CHAMPION	3rd place
1931-32	5-4	Runner-up (champion: Oklahoma)	
1932-33	4-0	Runner-up (champion: Iowa State)	
1933-34	4-5	4th place (champion: Oklahoma)	
1934-35	2-5	Runner-up (champion: Oklahoma)	
1935-36	5-2-1	3rd place (champion: Oklahoma)	
1936-37	4-7	Runner-up (champion: Iowa State)	7th place
1937-38	2-2-1	Runner-up (champion: Oklahoma)	
1938-39	5-5	CHAMPION	
1939-40	7-3-1	CHAMPION	
1940-41	6-5	Runner-up (champion: Iowa State)	8th place
1941-42	7-6	Runner-up (champion: Iowa State)	
1942-43	No team due to the WWII moratorium (Coach Patterson served in the U.S. Army)		
1943-44	No team due to the WWII moratorium (Coach Patterson served in the U.S. Army)		
1944-45	No team due to the WWII moratorium (Coach Patterson served in the U.S. Army)		
1945-46	No team due to the WWII moratorium (Coach Patterson served in the U.S. Army)		
1946-47	11-6	4th place (champion: Iowa State)	
Total	75-65-3		

Leon "Red" Reynard
Head Coach 1947-53
(six seasons)

Born: September 8, 1913 - Burr Oak, Kansas
Died: March 22, 2008 - Topeka, Kansas
Alma Mater: Kansas State University, 1940

Losing Coach Patterson only one season into the post-WWII "start-back" after four dormant seasons made it difficult for the Cats. Reynard came to the position with military experience and was a star on the gridiron as well as on the mat for the Cats, but K-State fell behind other programs that were moving into the modern era of college wrestling with more of a national recruiting focus, specialized training routines, and upgraded facilities. By all accounts, Reynard was cut out for the position, but the circumstances were not in his favor.

Season	Dual Record	Big 7 Conference finish
1947-48	3-8-1	4th place -first season for the Big 7- (champion: Oklahoma)
1948-49	2-10	4th place (champion: Nebraska, coached by Pat Patterson)
1949-50	1-7-2	4th place (champion: Oklahoma)
1950-51	3-6	Runner-up (champion: Oklahoma)
1951-52	5-3	5th place (champion: Oklahoma)
1952-53	3-6	3rd place (champion: Oklahoma)
Total	14-32-2	

Fritz Knorr

Head Coach: 1953-72

(19 seasons)

Born: May 9, 1907 - St. Joseph, Missouri
Died: Sept 9, 1972 - Savannah, Missouri
Alma Mater: Kansas State University, 1932

With Reynard's abrupt departure to enter private business, company man Fritz Knorr filled the void. Aside from a ten-year span after graduation when he coached and taught at the middle school, high school, and junior college levels, Knorr was associated with the university from 1927, when he entered as an undergrad, until his death in 1972.

He coached several sports and rose through the ranks in the athletic administration office, becoming assistant athletic director and business manager. Knorr also served on the NCAA Wrestling Rules Committee and worked to develop wrestling at the grassroots level in Kansas, where he was involved in coaching education and the promotion of youth wrestling. The Kansas Wrestling Coaches Association's (KWCA) annual fall clinic bears his name, "The KWCA Fritz Knorr Fall Clinic."

Season	Dual Record	Big 7 / Big 8 Conference finish
1953-54	5-4	4th place (champion: Oklahoma)
1954-55	4-5-1	4th place (champion: Oklahoma)
1955-56	5-4	3rd place (champion: Oklahoma)
1956-57	4-7	4th place -last season of Big 7 - (champion: Oklahoma)
1957-58	5-8	4th place -first season of Big 8 - (champion: Iowa State)
1958-59	5-10	5th place (champion: Oklahoma State)
1959-60	8-4	4th place (champion: Oklahoma)
1960-61	9-3	4th place (champion: Oklahoma State)
1961-62	4-9	6th place (champion: Oklahoma State)
1962-63	8-3	4th place (champion: Oklahoma State)
1963-64	6-5	5th place (champion: Oklahoma State)
1964-65	9-8-1	5th place (champion: Oklahoma State)
1965-66	7-7	6th place (champion: Oklahoma State)
1966-67	6-6	5th place (champion: Oklahoma)
1967-68	11-6-1	6th place (champion: tie Oklahoma, Oklahoma State)
1968-69	9-7	6th place (champion: Oklahoma State)
1969-70	6-8	4th place (champion: Iowa State)
1970-71	9-3	7th place (champion: Oklahoma State)
1971-72	5-8-1	7th place (champion: Oklahoma State)
Total	125-115-4	

Dale Samuelson

Head Coach 1972-73
(one season)

Born: Jan 4, 1950 - Colby, Kansas
Died: Feb 12, 2017 - Oakley, Kansas
Alma Mater: Kansas State University, 1972

Dale Samuelson, at only twenty-two years old, was thrust into an NCAA D1 head coaching position with no prior experience when Fritz Knorr passed away. Grad assistant one day, and head coach the next, was the progression for Samuelson.

Pressure on the K-State athletic administration, after it did not fund the trip to the 1973 NCAA tournament in Seattle, Washington for its three qualifiers, forced it to open the position to top college coaching candidates. Samuelson applied for the position but was passed over. He returned to his hometown of Oakley, where he had a long and productive career as a teacher and coach.

During his first season at Oakley High, the Plainsmen won the 1974 state championship in Class 2-1A. As of 2024, that is the only state wrestling title for OHS. All told, fourteen of his teams finished in the top-5 at State, including the title team and two teams that finished as runner-up (1993 and 1994).

Samuelson was inducted into the Kansas Wrestling Coaches Association Hall of Fame in 2006. He passed away in 2017.

Season	Dual Record	Big 8 Conference finish
1972-73	5-6	4th place (champion: Oklahoma State)

Fred Fozzard

Head Coach 1973-75

(two seasons)

Born: June 14, 1945 - Glenwood Springs, Colorado
Alma Mater: Oklahoma State University, 1968
Current Residence: La Pine, Oregon

After the negative attention that the school received as a result of Wayne Jackson hitchhiking to Seattle for the 1973 NCAA tournament, the athletic administration was pressured to search for a high-profile candidate rather than continue with Dale Samuelson, who was essentially handed the position weeks before the start of the 1972-73 season.

For the third time in program history, the K-State search led them to Stillwater and Oklahoma State University. The tradition, started by Ed Gallagher in the early 1900s, was still going strong, and a young, energetic candidate from the program was waiting for his turn to join the long list of former Cowboys to head up a D1 program.

Three-time All-American and 1967 NCAA champion Fred Fozzard fit the profile that Athletic Director Ernie Barrett was looking for. In addition to his college accolades, Fozzard was also a 1969 World champion and was currently serving as an assistant coach for Tommy Chesbro at OSU.

Fozzard was the head coach for only two seasons. His time in

Manhattan was marked by conflict with the administration and financial problems within the entire athletic department. He was fired in April of 1975, and the program was officially dropped in July, just three months later.

In 2012, Fozzard was inducted into the National Wrestling Hall of Fame as a Distinguished Member.

Season	Dual Record	Big 8 Conference finish
1973-74	7-9	4th place (champion: Oklahoma State)
1974-75	5-11	6th place (champion: Oklahoma State)

Appendix B: K-State Wrestling Rosters 1922-1975

It was not possible to include all of the K-State wrestling personalities and intriguing stories that come with them in this book. To honor all of the student-athletes who contributed to the program's history, the following is a compilation of each roster from the program's first year in 1922-23 to the final season in 1974-75. The list appears in alphabetical order with hometown and seasons of participation.

Every attempt was made to provide detailed and accurate information, but limitations were placed on what was available in *Royal Purple* yearbooks, local newspaper accounts, K-State *Collegiate* reporting, K-State student directories, and personal inquiries. All of these sources were tapped and carefully scrutinized. Cross-checks were made for spelling inconsistencies, use of casual and formal names, and dates. Hometowns were sometimes inconsistently reported. Where evidence was found to justify listing multiple locals, the primary was listed first, and secondary listings were placed in parentheses. The high school may also appear in parenthesis. A few wrestlers transferred in from other colleges and universities. Notations were made for that as well.

For many years, due to NCAA restrictions, freshmen were not included in "varsity" sports programs. For some years at K-State, freshmen were recorded as a separate entity, and in other years, not at all. In years where lists were available, the names were included. If verifiable evidence was not found, assumptions were not made, even in cases where sophomore, junior, and senior roster proof was found.

Putting the list together was neither easy nor straightforward, but it is as accurate as possible. If readers find possible omissions or inaccuracies, I welcome documentation that corrects the records.

The database contains 752 unique names. Analysis of the data shows some interesting trends and gives a snapshot of the program's deep history.

Student-athletes from twenty-five states and Washington DC were part of the K-State wrestling roster. Additionally, wrestlers from

Mexico and Peru were represented. However, 89 percent of participants hailed from the state of Kansas. Interestingly, not a single wrestler populated the cumulative roster from tradition-rich and nearby Iowa.

State/Country	# of wrestlers
Kansas	669
Oklahoma	17
Nebraska	10
New York	8
Missouri	7
Massachusetts	5
Illinois	4
California, Colorado, Minnesota, Pennsylvania	3
Idaho, South Dakota, Texas	2
AR, CT, DC, GA, HI, IN, MD, Mexico, MI, NJ, OR, Peru, WV, WI	1

K-State Wrestler	Hometown	State	Year 1	Year 2	Year 3	Year 4
Abel, Clarence	Oakley	KS	1937-38	1939-40		
Abernathy, Hugh (H.R.)	Manhattan	KS	1926-27	1928-29		
Ackerman, Fulton	Lincoln	KS	1929-30			
Adams, Dave	El Dorado	KS	1974-75			
Adams, Mike	Newton	KS	1974-75			
Adrian, Edgar	Burns	KS	1963-64			
Alder, Randall	Wellington	KS	1966-67			
Alexander, Arthur	Newton	KS	1973-74	1974-75		
Alexander, Roland	Wichita (North High)	KS	1952-53	1953-54	1954-55	1955-56
Allen, James	Newton	KS	1957-58			
Allen, Jerry	Canby	OR	1957-58	1958-59	1959-60	1960-61
Allen, Merle	Burlington	KS	1927-28	1928-29		
Alsop, Sam (S.E.)	Wakefield	KS	1928-29	1929-30	1934-35	
Ankenman, E.B.	Dellvale	KS	1928-29			
Armstrong, Bob	Omaha	NE	1937-38			
Arnett, Lawrence	Broughton	KS	1932-33			
Arnold, Darrell	Kansas City (Mission)	KS	1955-56			
Aschenbrenner, Frank	Colby	KS	1947-48	1948-49		
Atkinson, William	Hutchinson	KS	1963-64	1964-65		
Avery, Thomas	Coldwater	KS	1929-30			
Baker, Ron	Garden City	KS	1962-63	1963-64	1964-65	
Bangs, Fred	Madison	KS	1922-23			
Barber, Ben	Alton	KS	1928-29	1929-30	1930-31	
Barclay, Lyndsey	Topeka (West High)	KS	1974-75			

K-State Wrestler	Hometown	State	Year 1	Year 2	Year 3	Year 4
Barger, Jim	Blue Mound	KS	1938-39			
Barnes, Gregg	Newton	KS	1972-73	1973-74		
Barnes, Roby	Colby	KS	1956-57			
Barrett, James	Newton	KS	1966-67	1967-68	1968-69	1969-70
Bartlett, Ron	Junction City	KS	1973-74	1974-75		
Barton, Robert L.	Filer	ID	1929-30			
Beecroft, Kevin	Junction City	KS	1965-66			
Bellaire, Harold	Manhattan	KS	1946-47			
Berry, Darwin	Ponca City (Wilmot, KS)	OK	1934-35	1935-36	1936-37	1937-38
Betz, Elmer	Enterprise	KS	1935-36			
Bickel, Donald	Hoisington	KS	1946-47			
Bird, Alvin	Norton	KS	1960-61	1961-62	1962-63	
Bird, Larry	Norton	KS	1960-61	1961-62	1962-63	1963-64
Blanchard, Joe	Parsons	KS	1946-47	1947-48	1948-49	1949-50
Blasdel, H.P.	Herington	KS	1924-25			
Bliss, Robert	Atwood	KS	1964-65			
Blume, Dale	Atwood	KS	1954-55	1955-56	1956-57	
Bohnenblust, Howard	Leonardville	KS	1933-34			
Bond, G.T.	Topeka	KS	1924-24	1925-26		
Boon, Bill	Topeka	KS	1952-53			
Booth, Jim	Baldwin	KS	1956-57			
Boring, Warren	Kansas City	KS	1939-40	1940-41	1946-47	
Bowers, David	Herington	KS	1962-63			
Bowles, William	Inyokern	CA	1946-47			

K-State Wrestler	Hometown	State	Year 1	Year 2	Year 3	Year 4
Bozarth, Ferrell (F.M.)	Lenora	KS	1931-32	1932-33		
Bradshaw, John	Oakley	KS	1952-53	1953-54	1954-55	
Brandon, Glenn	Topeka	KS	1955-56	1956-57		
Brecheisen, Al	Rolla	KS	1941-42			
Bremner, Don	Orleans	MA	1946-47			
Brettschneider, Tom	Dundee	IL	1958-59			
Brinlee, Perry	Tulsa (Central High)	OK	1955-56	1956-57		
Broeckelman, Michael	Oakley	KS	1965-66			
Brown, Albert	Circleville	KS	1928-29			
Brown, Bill	Pittsburg	KS	1956-57			
Brown, Harry	Oberlin	KS	1936-37			
Brown, James	Los Angeles	CA	1937-38	1938-39	1939-40	
Brown, William	Larned	KS	1946-47	1947-48	1948-49	1949-50
Brown, William L.	Oberlin	KS	1964-65	1965-66	1966-67	1967-68
Brungardt, Mike	Garden City	KS	1972-73			
Buckmaster, A.D.	Manhattan	KS	1929-30			
Bukowski, Thomas	Russell	KS	1967-68			
Burbank, Wayne	Benton (Douglass)	KS	1931-32			
Burdo, Ben	Brooklyn	NY	1933-34	1934-35		
Burga, Manuel	Lambarque	Peru	1952-53			
Butler, Ben	Manhattan	KS	1932-33			
Byers, Larry	Salina	KS	1958-59	1959-60		
Campbell, Richard	Grenola	KS	1933-34	1934-35		
Campbell, Victor	Oakley	KS	1967-68			

K-State Wrestler	Hometown	State	Year 1	Year 2	Year 3	Year 4
Carleton, Edwin	Coldwater	KS	1948-49			
Carleton, Walter	Coldwater	KS	1933-34	1935-36	1936-37	1937-38
Carman, Melvin	St. Francis	KS	1966-67			
Carol, Edgar	Kansas City	KS	1957-58			
Carrell, Fred	Manhattan	KS	1956-57			
Carroll, Tim	Norton	KS	1962-63			
Carson, Jimmy	Winfield	KS	1949-50	1950-51		
Carter, Jon	Bethel (Kansas City)	KS	1966-67			
Case, Clifford	Coldwater	KS	1938-39	1940-41		
Caster, Jim	Douglass	KS	1955-56	1956-57	1957-58	1958-59
Caster, Larry	Douglass	KS	1957-58	1958-59	1960-61	1961-62
Cederberg, John	Herndon (Oberlin)	KS	1953-54			
Cederberg, Richard	Manhattan	KS	1948-49	1950-51		
Cervantez, Robert	Tulsa (Central High)	OK	1956-57	1957-58		
Chapman, Leo	Clay Center	KS	1938-39	1939-40		
Chapman, William	Wichita	KS	1928-29	1929-30	1930-31	
Chatfield, Elton	Goodland	KS	1953-54			
Cheynet, Jerry*	Wichita (Southeast High)	KS	1960-61	1962-63	1963-64	1964-65
Chronister, Paul	Abilene (Chapman)	KS	1938-39	1939-40	1941-42	
Clary, Bill	Kansas City	KS	1948-49			
Cleaver, T.	Iola	KS	1924-25			
Cole, Galen	Dodge City / DC Community College	KS	1974-75			
Coleman, Carol	Sylvia	KS	1935-36			

K-State Wrestler	Hometown	State	Year 1	Year 2	Year 3	Year 4
Coleman, John	Wichita (Cathedral High)	KS	1926-27			
Collins, Keith	Junction City	KS	1937-38	1939-40		
Coltrain, Wayne	Neodesha	KS	1946-47	1947-48		
Conrad, R.M.	Manhattan	KS	1929-30			
Cook, Albert	Haddam	KS	1924-25			
Cook, Lyle	St. Francis	KS	1965-66	1966-67	1968-69	1969-70
Cooper, Carleton	St. John	KS	1940-41			
Cordorelli, Augustus	Republic	PA	1933-34			
Cornell, Jack	Council Grove	KS	1934-35			
Couch, Charles	Kingsdown (Dodge City)	KS	1957-58	1958-59	1959-60	
Cox, Dale	Pauline	KS	1955-56			
Crackel, Gene	Hutchinson	KS	1946-47			
Cramer, Dick	Pratt / Pratt CC	KS	1973-74			
Crane, Eugene	Perry	OK	1969-70			
Creedon, Joe	Hyde Park	MA	1972-73			
Crews, Clarence	Elk Falls	KS	1924-25	1926-27	1927-28	
Criss, Gary	Manhattan	KS	1956-57	1957-58		
Crosby, Bill	Bellwood	IL	1973-74			
Crowley, John	Elkhart	KS	1936-37			
Curwell, Hugh	Wichita	KS	1938-39			
Dale, Ira (Lee)	Topeka	KS	1964-65	1965-66		
Dalton, Curtis (Elmer)	Webb City	OK	1949-50			
Dalton, Walter	Manhattan	KS	1947-48	1948-49	1949-50	
Daniels, Jesse	Douglass	KS	1954-55			

K-State Wrestler	Hometown	State	Year 1	Year 2	Year 3	Year 4
Darter, Don	Douglass	KS	1957-58	1958-59	1959-60	1960-61
Darter, Gary	Douglass	KS	1954-55	1955-56	1956-57	
Darter, Larry	Douglass	KS	1959-60			
Davies, Gordon H.	Manhattan	KS	1924-25			
Davies, K.L.	Emporia	KS	1932-33			
Davis, F.M.	Arkansas City	KS	1924-25			
DeBold, Patrick	Salina	KS	1971-72	1972-73		
Demo, Dan	El Dorado	KS	1974-75			
DeMoss, Richard, Jr.*	Wellington	KS	1960-61	1961-62	1962-63	1963-64
DeMoss, Richard, Sr.	Topeka (Topeka High)	KS	1935-36			
Dennison, H.M.	Berryton	KS	1924-25			
Dickson, Jaye	Stafford	KS	1970-71			
Dietrich, James*	Manhattan	KS	1955-56	1956-57	1957-58	1961-62
Donley, Phil	Douglass	KS	1972-73	1973-74		
Dooley, John	Wichita (Wichita East)	KS	1957-58	1958-59	1959-60	1960-61
Doyle, Bill (W.L.)	Douglass	KS	1926-27	1927-28	1930-31	1931-32
Doyle, Pat (John)	Douglass	KS	1955-56	1956-57	1957-58	1958-59
Dragone, Larry	Salina	KS	1966-67	1967-68	1970-71	
Dudgeon, Richard	Hebron	NE	1967-68			
Dudley, Max	Cawker City	KS	1939-40			
Duell, Ben	Goodland (Ruleton)	KS	1948-49	1949-50	1950-51	
Dukelow, Dave (D.B.)	Hutchinson	KS	1933-34	1934-35	1935-36	
Dukelow, John	Hutchinson	KS	1935-36			
Duncan, Clifford	St. Francis	KS	1935-36	1938-39		

K-State Wrestler	Hometown	State	Year 1	Year 2	Year 3	Year 4
Duncan, Dale	St. Francis	KS	1935-36	1936-37	1937-38	
Duncan, Glenn	St. Francis	KS	1936-37	1938-39	1939-40	1940-41
Duncan, Timothy	Manhattan	KS	1970-71			
Dunham, Daniel	Garden City	KS	1964-65			
Dunlap, Bob	Liberal	KS	1939-40	1940-41	1941-42	
Dunlap, S.N.	Berryton	KS	1924-25			
Dunlop, Robert	Liberal	KS	1941-42			
Durflinger, Glen	Arlington	KS	1946-47	1948-49		
Dwyer, Larry	Wellington	KS	1958-59			
Eads, James	Salina	KS	1957-58			
Edwards, Bill	Topeka (Bigelow, Irving)	KS	1959-60	1960-61		
Elder, Larry	Salina	KS	1964-65	1965-66	1966-67	1967-68
Elder, Steve	Salina	KS	1967-68	1968-69		
Ellegood, Ken	Oakley	KS	1954-55	1955-56		
Ellis, Ken*	Tulsa (Central High)	OK	1952-53	1953-54	1954-55	1955-56
Emmons, Perry	Lenora	KS	1941-42			
Engel, R.E.	Hope	KS	1924-25			
Engelage, Paul	Lockwood	MO	1949-50			
Epler, W.N.	Scott City	KS	1929-30			
Ernest, Leon	Stockton	KS	1956-57			
Errington, Hugh "Duke" (C.H.)	Ruleton (Goodland)	KS	1927-28	1928-29	1929-30	1930-31
Eschbaugh, Clifford Wayne	Manhattan	KS	1922-23			
Etherton, David	Marysville	KS	1973-74			
Etrick, M.M.	Dodge City	KS	1924-25			

K-State Wrestler	Hometown	State	Year 1	Year 2	Year 3	Year 4
Everist, Pete (Marvin)	Oberlin	KS	1954-55	1955-56	1956-57	1957-58
Falwell, Ralph	Kansas City	KS	1946-47	1947-48	1948-49	
Falwell, Warren	Kansas City	KS	1948-49			
Fanning, Paul	Melvern	KS	1933-34			
Fansher, Farland	Edmond	OK	1935-36	1937-38	1938-39	1939-40
Fansher, Forrest	Edmond	OK	1933-34	1934-35	1935-36	1937-38
Fansher, Marvin	Edmond	OK	1948-49			
Fansher, Stan	Edmond	OK	1946-47	1947-48	1948-49	
Farley, Terry	Hutchinson	KS	1973-74	1974-75		
Faulconer, (G.H.) Guy	El Dorado	KS	1923-24	1924-25		
Felton, Richard	Junction City	KS	1973-74			
Fergerson, Steve	Dodge City	KS	1968-69	1969-70	1970-71	1971-72
Fettes, John	Colby	KS	1959-60	1960-61	1961-62	
Fettes, Joseph J.	Romeo	CO	1962-63	1963-64		
Fickel, Joe (J.C.)	Chanute	KS	1929-30	1930-31	1928-29	
Fields, William	Salina	KS	1965-66	1966-67	1967-68	
Figge, Fred	Wheaton	KS	1953-54			
Figgs, Larry	Valley Falls	KS	1955-56			
Fisher, Roger	Norton	KS	1970-71	1971-72	1972-73	1973-74
Fixen, Richard	Goodland	KS	1949-50	1954-55	1955-56	
Fleck, R.W.	Beloit	KS	1928-29			
Flipse, W.	Manhattan	KS	1924-25			
Flowers, Ricky	Ulysses	KS	1971-72			
Foland, Merle	Almena	KS	1937-38			

K-State Wrestler	Hometown	State	Year 1	Year 2	Year 3	Year 4
Foos, Fred	Great Bend	KS	1972-73			
Fortune, Cedric	Garden City	KS	1958-59			
Foss, W.D.	Manhattan	KS	1922-23			
Foster, Bob	Wichita (North High)	KS	1954-55			
Fowler, Dick	Holton	KS	1933-34			
Frakes, Charlie	Douglass	KS	1973-74			
Fraser, Stanley (S.M.)	Talmadge (Abilene)	KS	1924-25	1925-26	1926-27	
Frey, Cullen G.	Manhattan	KS	1922-23	1923-24		
Frey, Larry	Abilene	KS	1955-56			
Freytag, Dale	Goodland	KS	1954-55			
Frisbie, G.D.	Abilene	KS	1924-25			
Fritzmeyer, B.	Stafford	KS	1924-25			
Fudim, Murray	Westbury	NY	1956-57			
Funk, Otto (O.R.)	Marion	KS	1928-29			
Furtick, Don	Salina	KS	1946-47			
Gallaway, Dale	Topeka	KS	1973-74	1974-75		
Garcia, Ron	Douglass	KS	1973-74			
Garcia, Rosalio "Gus"*	Douglass	KS	1959-60	1960-61	1961-62	1962-63
Gard, Dee	Goodland	KS	1957-58	1958-59	1959-60	1960-61
Gartner, John F.	Manhattan	KS	1922-23			
Gee, Jerry	Stafford	KS	1968-69	1969-70		
Germann, H.I.	Fairview	KS	1927-28			
Gerstner, Don	Medicine Lodge (Sharon)	KS	1949-50	1950-51		
Gilkison, Rich	Effingham	KS	1962-63			

K-State Wrestler	Hometown	State	Year 1	Year 2	Year 3	Year 4
Gilmore, Lloyd	Independence	KS	1956-57			
Gilmore, Melvin	Selkirk	KS	1946-47			
Glace, William	Oneida (Bern High)	KS	1965-66			
Glaze, Ray	Baltimore	MD	1954-55	1955-56	1956-57	1957-58
Glenn, Bill	Topeka (Hayden High)	KS	1966-67			
Godney, B.	Concordia	KS	1924-25			
Gollier, Terry	Independence	KS	1955-56			
Gonzales, Frank	Bonner Springs / Santa Ana (CA) Junior College	KS	1974-75			
Good, Jim	Salina	KS	1955-56			
Goodrich, E.G.	Goodland	KS	1922-23			
Goreham, Ken	Junction City	KS	1964-65			
Gosney, William (W.W.)	Goddard	KS	1927-28	1928-29		
Gramzoe, Bob	Almena	KS	1954-55			
Grant, Russell	Wichita (West High)	KS	1956-57	1957-58		
Greene, David	El Dorado	KS	1964-65			
Gregg, Vaughn	Hiawatha	KS	1948-49			
Grentz, Glen	Tampa	KS	1936-37			
Griffith, Paul	Edmond	OK	1929-30	1930-31	1932-33	1933-34
Grove, John (Jack)	Hutchinson (Westminster, CA)	KS	1960-61	1959-60	1961-62	1962-63
Gugle, Terry	Holdrege	NE	1967-68			
Guinn, Don	Oberlin	KS	1956-57			
Gull, Chester (C.N.)	El Dorado	KS	1935-36			
Gump, Robert	Abilene	KS	1929-30			

K-State Wrestler	Hometown	State	Year 1	Year 2	Year 3	Year 4
Hackney, Elmer	Oberlin	KS	1936-37	1937-38	1938-39	
Hackney, Gerald	Oberlin	KS	1947-48	1948-49		
Halbower, Charles	Anthony	KS	1946-47			
Hale, Steve	St. Francis	KS	1972-73			
Haller, Gary	Colby	KS	1954-55	1955-56	1956-57	1957-58
Hambleton, James	Hutchinson	KS	1973-74			
Hamby, Dan	Hutchinson	KS	1974-75			
Hammerschmidt, Neil	Hays	KS	1969-70	1970-71		
Hancock, John	St. Francis	KS	1938-39	1940-41		
Haney, Michael	Kansas City (Turner High)	KS	1966-67			
Hansen, Dwaine	Minneola	KS	1957-58			
Hanson, F.V.	Concordia	KS	1922-23			
Hanson, Jay	Independence	KS	1948-49	1949-50		
Hardin, Daslie	Kansas City	KS	1966-67			
Hardtafred, O.M.	Lawrence	KS	1929-30			
Harner, J.E.	Keats	KS	1922-23			
Harrington, Ed "Skippy"	Wichita (East High)	KS	1954-55	1955-56		
Harris, Tony (Antonio M.)	Junction City	KS	1972-73			
Harrison, John	Alden (Sterling)	KS	1935-36	1936-37		
Hartman, William	Hoxie	KS	1938-39	1939-40		
Hawk, Thomas	Colby	KS	1966-67			
Hayden, John	Twin Falls	ID	1938-39			
Haynes, Gerald	Douglass	KS	1965-66			
Headley, Jack	Wichita	KS	1955-56			

K-State Wrestler	Hometown	State	Year 1	Year 2	Year 3	Year 4
Healy, Mike	Wichita	KS	1958-59			
Hecker, Virgil	Oakley	KS	1954-55			
Hedlund, Jay	Overland Park	KS	1965-66			
Heermance, Jan	Manhattan	KS	1965-66			
Hegberg, William	Bellevue	NE	1964-65			
Heit, Michael	Kinsley	KS	1970-71			
Helm, Adolph	Chanute	KS	1924-25			
Hemmerling, Dwight*	Hutchinson	KS	1966-67	1967-68	1968-69	1969-70
Hendricks, R.D	Wakeeny	KS	1922-23			
Hendrix, Joe J.	Lone	KS	1925-26			
Henry, Allan	Colby	KS	1955-56			
Herr, H.K.	Manhattan	KS	1925-26			
Hess, Dean	Colby	KS	1946-47	1947-48	1948-49	
Hicks, T.W.	Norton	KS	1922-23			
Higgins, Darrell	Tulsa	OK	1956-57	1958-59		
Hightower, Curt	Wichita (Kapaun High)	KS	1973-74			
Hilding, Eric	Wichita (Kapaun High)	KS	1972-73			
Hinkle, Clifford N.	Lenora	KS	1926-27	1927-28		
Hinkle, R.	Carbondale	KS	1931-32			
Hinkson, Newt	Halstead	KS	1933-34			
Hinz, E.L.	Abilene	KS	1932-33			
Hinz, Walter (W.H.)	Abilene	KS	1923-24	1924-25	1925-26	1926-27
Hodges, Larry	Goodland	KS	1955-56	1956-57		
Hodgson, Bob	Manhattan	KS	1954-55			

K-State Wrestler	Hometown	State	Year 1	Year 2	Year 3	Year 4
Hogan, Michael	Manhattan	KS	1969-70			
Holder, Richard	Uniontown	KS	1946-47			
Holland, R.B. (Rolla)	Iola	KS	1933-34	1934-35	1935-36	
Holliman, Terry	St. Francis	KS	1970-71	1971-72		
Hooper, Mark	Owl's Head	NY	1954-55			
Hopeman, Victor	Independence	KS	1932-33			
Horning, James	Almena	KS	1962-63	1963-64	1964-65	
Horton, Tommy	Topeka	KS	1962-63			
Hostetter, Jim	Manhattan	KS	1955-56	1956-57		
Houser, Ed	Douglass (Rock/Udall)	KS	1932-33	1933-34		
Howard, Charles	Salina	KS	1967-68	1968-69	1969-70	
Howard, Ralph	Mount Hope	KS	1924-25			
Howard, Richard	Douglass	KS	1965-66			
Howe, Eugene (E.E.)	Stockton	KS	1932-33	1933-34	1934-35	1935-36
Howell, Lewis	Norton	KS	1946-47			
Howell, Richard	Louisburg	KS	1964-65			
Hraba, Adolph	East St. Louis	IL	1929-30			
Hubbard, E.F.	Linwood	KS	1926-27			
Hueftle, Mark	Oakley	KS	1955-56			
Huggins, Darrell	Tulsa	OK	1956-57	1957-58	1959-60	1960-61
Hughes, Gary	Lyons	KS	1954-55			
Hume, J.N.	Humboldt	KS	1922-23			
Hunter, John	Sun City	KS	1948-49			
Hurlock, Wyndon	St. Francis	KS	1935-36			

K-State Wrestler	Hometown	State	Year 1	Year 2	Year 3	Year 4
Hurtt, James	Colby	KS	1956-57	1957-58		
Huyeck, K.R.	Morrowville	KS	1928-29	1929-30		
Hyde, King	Altoona	KS	1955-56			
Ireland, Bob	Valley Center	KS	1959-60	1960-61		
Isabella, Lou	Scotia	NY	1949-50			
Jabara, George	Wichita (Heights High)	KS	1966-67			
Jackson, Mark	Arkansas City	KS	1971-72	1972-73	1973-74	1974-75
Jackson, Wayne*	Arkansas City	KS	1969-70	1970-71	1971-72	1972-73
Jacobson, David	Brooklyn	NY	1936-37	1937-38		
James, Larry	Wichita (South High)	KS	1964-65	1965-66		
Jessup, Ernest	Wichita (East High)	KS	1933-34	1934-35	1935-36	1936-37
Johnson, Bob	Hutchinson	KS	1941-42	1946-47		
Johnson, J.H.	Norton	KS	1924-25			
Johnson, Walter	Emmett	KS	1938-39			
Jones, Edward	El Dorado	KS	1955-56			
Jones, Floyd	Leavenworth	KS	1964-65			
Jones, R.V.	Manhattan	KS	1928-29			
Jones, Terron	Junction City (Ft. Riley)	KS	1965-66	1966-67		
Kadel, John	Wichita (Height High) / OU	KS	1973-74			
Kail, Richard	St. Francis	KS	1955-56			
Kastner, Bill	Salina	KS	1956-57	1957-58	1958-59	
Keith, Arlen	Salina	KS	1959-60	1960-61	1961-62	1962-63
Keller, Dan	St. Francis	KS	1972-73			
Keller, Dick	St. Francis	KS	1972-73			

K-State Wrestler	Hometown	State	Year 1	Year 2	Year 3	Year 4
Keller, Ed	St. Francis	KS	1935-36	1936-37	1937-38	1938-39
Keller, Elton	St. Francis	KS	1948-49			
Keller, Thomas	St. Francis	KS	1966-67	1967-68	1968-69	1969-70
Keller, William	St. Francis	KS	1968-69	1969-70	1970-71	1971-72
Kelley, Charles	Norcatur	KS	1959-60	1961-62		
Kelley, James	Norcatur	KS	1958-59			
Kent, James	Norton	KS	1964-65			
Kepley, L.F.	Chanute	KS	1928-29	1929-30		
Kimball, Donald	Lane	KS	1939-40			
Kimball, Keith	Manhattan	KS	1929-30			
King, Tom	Douglass	KS	1955-56	1956-57		
Kirk, Bob	Scott City	KS	1932-33			
Kleiss, Leslie (L.D.)	Coffeyville	KS	1930-31			
Knedlick, Ralph	Belleville	KS	1936-37			
Knight, Jerry	Topeka	KS	1959-60			
Knorr, Fred	Manhattan	KS	1955-56			
Knorr, Fritz (F.C.)	Savannah	MO	1927-28	1928-29	1930-31	
Knorr, William	Manhattan	KS	1966-67	1970-71		
Knowlton, Richard	Oxford	KS	1946-47			
Kramer, Leslie	Vermillion (Lillis)	KS	1949-50	1950-51	1951-52	1952-53
Krannawitter, Oliver	Hoxie	KS	1966-67			
Kraus, W.J.	Hays	KS	1924-25			
Kriss, Joel	Colby	KS	1964-65			
LaCross, Gregg	Wichita (Heights High)	KS	1966-67			

K-State Wrestler	Hometown	State	Year 1	Year 2	Year 3	Year 4
Lamb, E.R.	Mendon	MO	1931-32	1932-33		
Lampe, Daniel	St. Francis	KS	1957-58			
Landes, Marvin	Wellington	KS	1966-67	1967-68	1968-69	
Landholm, Joe	Oakland	NE	1953-54	1954-55	1955-56	
Landon, W.E.	Mayetta	KS	1924-25			
Langford (Moyer), Robert	Jonesboro	AR	1949-50			
Langhofer, Bill	Plains	KS	1948-49			
Lankas, Daniel	Atwood	KS	1965-66			
Latimer, K.J.	Humboldt	KS	1928-29	1929-30		
Laughlin, Jim	Goodland	KS	1954-55			
Lawrence, Thomas	Wichita	KS	1961-62			
Lay, Russell	Port Washington	NY	1964-65	1965-66	1966-67	
LeClare, J.B.	Coffeyville	KS	1932-33			
Lee, Dale	Topeka (Highland Park)	KS	1965-66			
Lee, David	Honolulu	HI	1962-63			
Lehner, John	Newton	KS	1960-61			
Lehr, Robert	Wichita	KS	1966-67			
Leimbrock, Freddie	Wichita (East High)	KS	1935-36	1936-37		
Lesher, Clark	Borger	TX	1952-53			
Lester, Stephen	Wichita (North High)	KS	1957-58			
LeVitt, Gray	Ellsworth	KS	1924-25			
Liebler, Al	Manhattan	KS	1954-55	1955-56		
Lightner, David	Garden City	KS	1964-65	1965-66	1966-67	1967-68
Lindsay, D.J.	Madison	KS	1924-25			

K-State Wrestler	Hometown	State	Year 1	Year 2	Year 3	Year 4
Linnell, James	Goodland	KS	1949-50	1954-55	1955-56	
Linnell, Lyle	Goodland	KS	1948-49	1949-50	1950-51	1951-52
List, Martin	Norborne	MO	1964-65			
Little, Martin	Douglass	KS	1962-63	1963-64	1964-65	1965-66
Livingston, Charles	Manhattan	KS	1959-60			
Lobenstein, H.L.	Bonner Springs	KS	1922-23	1923-24	1924-25	1925-26
Lockstrom, Don	Salina (Solomon)	KS	1947-48	1948-49	1949-50	1951-52
Logan, B.B.	Towanda	KS	1922-23			
Long, David	Topeka (West High)	KS	1974-75			
Long, George (G.W.) "Shorty"	Burlington	KS	1927-28	1929-30		
Lotta, Robert	Holton	KS	1933-34			
Lovin, Robert	Hoxie	KS	1956-57	1957-58		
Lowenheimer, L.	Leavenworth	KS	1924-25			
Lowman, Tom	Manhattan	KS	1959-60			
Lowry, Myron	Norton	KS	1967-68	1968-69		
Lummio, Al	East Chicago (Washington High)	IN	1948-49			
Lundberg, Jim	Manhattan	KS	1966-67	1972-73		
Lundy, Tom	Salina	KS	1959-60	1960-61		
Lundy, William	Salina	KS	1965-66			
Lyons, Charles	Kansas City	KS	1946-47	1947-48	1948-49	
Machart, Michael	Oberlin	KS	1962-63	1963-64		
Macias, R.V.	Yacatecas	Mexico	1924-25			
Madden, Barry	Norton	KS	1970-71	1971-72		
Mader, Lyle	Edgemont	SD	1946-47			

K-State Wrestler	Hometown	State	Year 1	Year 2	Year 3	Year 4
Maestas, Alan	Derby	KS	1967-68	1968-69	1969-70	1970-71
Mancuso, Bob*	Omaha (Central High)	NE	1951-52	1952-53	1953-54	1954-55
Mannebach, Alfred	Hoxie	KS	1958-59			
Mantz, C.E.	Pratt	KS	1929-30			
Marciniak, Ron	Pittsburgh	PA	1952-53	1953-54		
Marquez, Ramon	Mulvane	KS	1939-40			
Marsh, O.E.	Fort Scott	KS	1924-25			
Martin, Don	Clay Center	KS	1955-56	1956-57		
Martin, Phil	Clay Center	KS	1969-70	1972-73		
Martinez, Albert	Newton	KS	1962-63			
Marx, E.P.	Manhattan	KS	1932-33			
Matney, Clayton	Larned	KS	1935-36			
May, Tony (Edward)	Derby	KS	1973-74	1974-75		
Mayer, Bob	Brewster	KS	1949-50	1950-51		
Mayhew, Jay	Belpre (Trusdale)	KS	1936-37			
Mayo, Jim	Wichita (East High)	KS	1952-53			
McCaskill, George	Kansas City	KS	1946-47			
McCaslin, Wayne	Osborne	KS	1926-27	1927-28	1928-29	
McClellan, Verle (V.O.)*	Wichita (East High)	KS	1938-39	1939-40	1940-41	1946-47
McCloskey, John	Salina	KS	1967-68	1968-69		
McClung, Mickey	Goodland	KS	1960-61			
McCosh, Gordon	Abilene	KS	1965-66			
McCutchen, Elvis	Kingman	KS	1938-39			
McDaniel, Denny	Tulsa	OK	1952-53			

K-State Wrestler	Hometown	State	Year 1	Year 2	Year 3	Year 4
McDonald, Alvin (A.R.)	Bremen	KS	1932-33	1933-34		
McDonald, Ed	Peabody	MA	1937-38			
McDougal, James	Atwood (Ludell)	KS	1965-66	1966-67	1967-68	1968-69
McElwee, Virgil	Kansas City	KS	1962-63			
McGee, D.W.	Liberal	KS	1931-32			
McGrew, Victor	Merriam	KS	1954-55			
McHenry, Wendell	Meriden	KS	1956-57			
McJunkin, Daniel	Topeka (Topeka High)	KS	1962-63	1963-64		
McKibben, Roy (R.H.)	Kansas City	KS	1927-28	1928-29	1929-30	
McKnight, E.B.	Eskridge	KS	1924-25			
McKoon, Allen	Osawatomie	KS	1970-71			
McLachlan, Dan	Pleasanton	KS	1928-29			
McMullen, Phillip	Stella	NE	1927-27			
McNeal, James D.	Wayzata	MN	1960-61			
McRae, Denzil	Altamont	KS	1948-49	1949-50		
McWilliams, Jerry	Topeka	KS	1954-55			
Melia, L.E.	Ford	KS	1926-27	1927-28		
Mendelsohn, Barry	Huntington Station	NY	1973-74			
Merriman, George	Carsonville	MI	1939-40			
Merritt, Chuck	Newton	KS	1972-73	1973-74		
Metz, Jerry	Douglass (Wichita)	KS	1961-62	1962-63	1963-64	
Meyer, Charles	Manhattan	KS	1970-71	1971-72		
Miller, Frank	Manhattan	KS	1970-71	1971-72		
Miller, J.M.	Sycamore	KS	1931-32			

K-State Wrestler	Hometown	State	Year 1	Year 2	Year 3	Year 4
Miller, James (Riley)	Wichita (North High)	KS	1955-56	1956-57	1957-58	1958-59
Miller, James R.	Newton	KS	1966-67			
Miller, Jerry	Norton	KS	1970-71			
Miller, Joyce	Sycamore	KS	1932-33			
Miller, Keith	Dellvale	KS	1937-38			
Miller, L.C.	Norton	KS	1924-25			
Mills, Bill	Olathe	KS	1954-55	1956-57		
Mills, Kenneth	Neodesha	KS	1946-47			
Mills, Lee	St. Francis	KS	1949-50	1950-51		
Mines, Keith	Oberlin (Cedar Bluffs)	KS	1948-49			
Mines, Kyle	Oberlin (Cedar Bluffs)	KS	1948-49	1953-54	1954-55	1955-56
Mitchem, John	Sedgwick	KS	1964-65			
Mogusar, Dennis	Louisburg	KS	1965-66			
Moody, Ed	Greeley	KS	1931-32			
Moore, Walter	Dresden	KS	1939-40			
Morford, Gene	Oberlin	KS	1964-65			
Morgan, Rodney	El Dorado	KS	1967-68	1968-69		
Morris, H.O.	Mount Hope	KS	1924-25			
Morton, Dick	Goodland	KS	1951-52			
Mosa, Joe	Clinton	MA	1949-50	1950-51	1951-52	
Moser, Michael	Oakley	KS	1962-63	1964-65		
Mosier, Frank	Hoxie	KS	1948-49			
Munson, James	Arkansas City	KS	1965-66			
Murphy, George (R.P.)	Lincoln (Norton)	KS	1931-32	1932-33		

K-State Wrestler	Hometown	State	Year 1	Year 2	Year 3	Year 4
Neff, Arthur	Solomon	KS	1939-40			
Nelson, Paul	Atwood	KS	1972-73	1973-74	1974-75	
Nichols, William	Waterville	KS	1938-39			
Nighswonger, Charles	St. Francis	KS	1946-47	1947-48	1948-49	
Noe, Danny	Topeka	KS	1955-56	1956-57	1958-59	
Norton, Kenneth	Oberlin (Lebanon)	KS	1936-37	1937-38		
Nuttle, Dave	El Dorado	KS	1954-55	1955-56	1956-57	
O'Neal, George	Colby	KS	1947-48	1948-49		
Ogden, Alvin	Lyons	KS	1949-50	1950-51	1951-52	
Olsen, Rod	Abilene	KS	1966-67			
Ottenberg, Ray	Washington	DC	1964-65			
Pacha, Leonard	Marysville	KS	1950-51	1951-52	1952-53	1953-54
Paddleford, Don	Manhattan	KS	1935-36			
Page, Bernie	Wichita (Southeast)	KS	1967-68	1969-70		
Paige, Orville	Manhattan	KS	1946-47			
Parks, Wendell	Wichita (East High)	KS	1949-50			
Patterson, Herman	Lorraine	KS	1946-47			
Patterson, Merle "Bud"	Manhattan	KS	1931-32			
Patterson, Ray	Derby	KS	1966-67			
Patterson, Raymond	Morrowville	KS	1928-29	1929-30		
Paulsen, Cecil	Onega	KS	1940-41			
Payne, Jay	Delphos	KS	1937-38	1938-39		
Paynter, Raymond (R.C.)	Manhattan	KS	1926-27	1927-28	1928-29	
Peal, H.H.	Augusta	KS	1924-25			

K-State Wrestler	Hometown	State	Year 1	Year 2	Year 3	Year 4
Pearson, Zurlinden L.	Manhattan	KS	1924-25	1925-26		
Perine, Jack	Wamego	KS	1946-47			
Pescador, Jesus	Lincoln	KS	1953-54			
Peterson, Bob	Kansas City	KS	1935-36			
Peterson, Charles	Junction City	KS	1961-62			
Peterson, K.E.	Enterprise	KS	1924-25			
Pfizenmaier, Scott	Clay Center	KS	1973-74			
Pfuetze, Paul	Manhattan	KS	1924-25	1925-26		
Pierce, L.D.	Scranton	KS	1928-29			
Pierce, R.	Lucas	KS	1928-29			
Pierson, Bruce	Clay Center	KS	1967-68			
Pike, Ross	Wichita (North High)	KS	1955-56	1957-58		
Portenier, H.E.	Phillipsburg	KS	1923-24			
Porter, Armer	Manhattan	KS	1922-23			
Porter, Jerald G.	Dellvale (Norton)	KS	1938-39	1939-40	1940-41	1941-42
Porter, Leland	Dellvale (Norton)	KS	1937-38	1938-39	1939-40	1940-41
Potter, Thomas	Upper Darby	PA	1955-56			
Rainer, Daryl	Wichita (West High)	KS	1965-66			
Rainsberger, Ellis	East St. Louis	IL	1954-55	1955-56	1956-57	
Randall, Bruce	Perry	OK	1973-74	1974-75		
Randle, E.W.	Jefferson	KS	1928-29	1929-30		
Rawlins, R.L.	Whiting	KS	1928-29			
Reber, R.D.	Morrill	KS	1924-25			
Reece, Adelbert Samuel	Manhattan	KS	1922-23			

K-State Wrestler	Hometown	State	Year 1	Year 2	Year 3	Year 4
Reed, Myron	Norton	KS	1926-27			
Regnier, E.H.	Spearville	KS	1929-30			
Reid, James	Manhattan	KS	1928-29			
Reinhert, Gary	Atwood	KS	1971-72			
Rempe, Ken	Plainville	KS	1967-68			
Reynard, Jerry	Manhattan	KS	1959-60			
Reynard, Leon "Red"	Alamo (Topeka, Manhattan, KS)	TX	1936-37	1937-38	1938-39	1939-40
Rhoades, Glen	Manhattan	KS	1922-23	1923-24		
Richards, Gary	Oberlin	KS	1966-67	1967-68	1968-69	1969-70
Richardson, Dale	Hoxie	KS	1949-50			
Richardson, Jack	Cameron	MO	1958-59			
Richardson, James L.	Stafford	KS	1966-67			
Richardson, John	Dodge City	KS	1926-27	1927-28	1930-31	
Richardson, Wayne	Goodland	KS	1949-50	1950-51		
Riddell, John	Salina	KS	1948-49	1949-50		
Rieke, Duane	Republic (Vattier)	KS	1949-50	1950-51	1951-52	
Rieniets, David	Wichita (South High)	KS	1965-66			
Rippe, Bob	Ludell (Atwood)	KS	1958-59			
Risley, Ivan	Nickerson	KS	1948-49			
Ritterhouse, Tom	Salina	KS	1955-56			
Roberts, Jim	Tulsa (Central High)	OK	1955-56	1956-57		
Roberts, June	Ford	KS	1930-31	1931-32	1932-33	
Rogers, Cecil	Bethel	KS	1949-50	1950-51		
Rogers, Dan	Topeka (Seaman High)	KS	1972-73			

K-State Wrestler	Hometown	State	Year 1	Year 2	Year 3	Year 4
Rokey, Ray	Sebetha	KS	1941-42			
Romero, Ray	Wichita (North High)	KS	1946-47			
Romine, F.W. (Floyd)	Osage City	KS	1926-27			
Ross, E.L.	Ashland	KS	1928-29			
Roswurm, Richard C.	Colorado Springs	CO	1966-67			
Ruda, Dan	Atwood	KS	1972-73	1973-74		
Ruda, Frank	Atwood	KS	1939-40			
Ruffino, Thomas	Omaha	NE	1964-65			
Ruhlman, Tom	Atchison	KS	1955-56			
Russell, Ralph	Bucyrus	KS	1954-55			
Russell, Roy	Climax	KS	1955-56			
Sabin, Paul	Salina	KS	1955-56	1956-57		
Sammons, Ted	Stockton	KS	1948-49	1949-50		
Sampson, Raymond	Severy	KS	1946-47			
Samuelson, Dale	Oakley / Colby CC	KS	1970-71	1971-72		
Santiago, Steve	Wichita (North High)	KS	1955-56			
Scannell, Steve	Lawrence	KS	1972-73			
Scheer, Paul	Marion	KS	1937-38			
Scheneberger, Edward	Cuba	KS	1924-25			
Schlaefli, Lyle	Cawker City	KS	1935-36			
Schmidt, Gregg	Rockham	SD	1966-67			
Schmidt, O.D.	Lorraine	KS	1924-25			
Schmidt, Robert	Caldwell	KS	1955-56	1956-57		
Schmidt, Wolfgang	Paola	KS	1964-65			

K-State Wrestler	Hometown	State	Year 1	Year 2	Year 3	Year 4
Schofield, John	Walnut Creek	CA	1964-65	1965-66		
Schoop, Fred (Ralph)	Abilene	KS	1924-25	1925-26	1926-27	
Schottler, Kirk	Wichita (South High)	KS	1974-75			
Schottler, Mark	Wichita (South High)	KS	1974-75			
Schreiner, Leslie	Douglass	KS	1962-63	1963-64	1964-65	1965-66
Schroeder, Nicholas	Colby	KS	1954-55	1955-56		
Schruben, M	Dresden	KS	1929-30			
Schubert, C.A.	Centralia	KS	1929-30			
Schuff, R.	Abilene	KS	1924-25			
Schwalbe, Calvin	Waconia	MN	1954-55	1956-57		
Scott, F.E.	Independence	KS	1924-25			
Scott, Kenneth	Kalvesta	KS	1961-62			
Scott, W.S.	Ellis	KS	1924-25			
Seay, Joe	Wellington	KS	1958-59	1960-61	1961-62	1962-63
Shadid, James	Wichita (Southeast)	KS	1962-63			
Sharp, Mark	Manhattan	KS	1964-65			
Sharp, Richard	Wichita (East High)	KS	1948-49			
Shaw, Ken	Charleston	WV	1956-57			
Shay, Larry	Tecumseh	KS	1965-66			
Sheets, Dean	Burlington	KS	1949-50	1950-51	1951-52	
Sheets, Larry	Topeka	KS	1960-61	1961-62		
Sherar, Willard J. "Pete"*	Latham	KS	1932-33	1933-34	1934-35	1935-36
Sherwood, K.M.	Concordia	KS	1927-28	1928-29		
Shideler, F.M.	Girard	KS	1924-25			

K-State Wrestler	Hometown	State	Year 1	Year 2	Year 3	Year 4
Shier, W.D.	Gypsum	KS	1933-34			
Sides, Keith	Norton	KS	1974-75			
Simonton, Charles	Oakley	KS	1955-56			
Simpson, Dale	Oberlin	KS	1946-47			
Skelton, Tom	Goodland	KS	1954-55			
Slocombe, L.D.	Peabody	KS	1924-25			
Smerchek, J.D.	Garnett	KS	1929-30			
Smith, C.F.	Beloit	KS	1924-25			
Smith, Denton	Russell	KS	1960-61	1961-62	1962-63	1963-64
Smith, Gerald	Houston	KS	1954-55			
Smith, John	Junction City	KS	1966-67			
Smith, Kenneth	Newton	KS	1969-70	1970-71		
Smith, Loren	Ponca City (El Dorado, KS)	OK	1934-35	1935-36	1936-37	
Smith, Ray	Topeka (Seaman High)	KS	1964-65			
Smith, Roscoe	El Dorado (Ponca City, OK)	KS	1936-37	1937-38		
Smith, Tom L	Parsons	KS	1948-49			
Snyder, Veryle	Mayetta	KS	1941-42			
Solomon, Frank	Yates Center (Wichita)	KS	1947-48	1948-49	1949-50	1950-51
Son, Keven	Fredonia	KS	1974-75			
Soupene, Bill	Manhattan	KS	1959-60			
Spear, David	Norton	KS	1972-73			
Spicher, Ken	Glasco	KS	1952-53	1953-54	1954-55	
Spring, Richard	St. John	KS	1952-53			
Sprinkle, Chuck	Hutchinson	KS	1955-56			

K-State Wrestler	Hometown	State	Year 1	Year 2	Year 3	Year 4
Stafford, Jeff	Kansas City	KS	1972-73			
Standley, C.A.	Lucas	KS	1928-29			
Stanley, Earl (Wayne)	Douglass	KS	1958-59	1959-60	1960-61	1961-62
Stanley, Jim	Oberlin	KS	1971-72			
Stark, Eugene (Henry)	Harper	KS	1946-47			
Stark, H.H.	Wellington	KS	1932-33			
Sterling, Joe	Iola (Humboldt)	KS	1949-50	1950-51		
Stewart, H.A.	Abilene	KS	1924-25			
Stiefel, Melvin	Gypsum	KS	1941-42			
Stivers, Fred	Rome	GA	1962-63	1963-64		
Stoneking, E.L.	Baldwin	KS	1929-30			
Stover, Harold	Goddard	KS	1926-27			
Strasser, Alvin	Goodland	KS	1973-74			
Stroble, John	Newton	KS	1974-75			
Stroh, Bob	Hartford	CT	1959-60			
Stueve, Carl	Olpe	KS	1968-69	1969-70		
Stueve, Clint	Emporia	KS	1974-75			
Stueve, Doug	Olpe	KS	1968-69	1969-70	1970-71	1971-72
Stumbo, R.W.	Bayard	KS	1928-29			
Sudduth, Scottie	Wichita	KS	1961-62			
Swift, Dean E.	Olathe (Ft. Smith, AR)	KS	1931-32	1932-33	1933-34	1934-35
Switzky, Dennis	Topeka	KS	1969-70	1970-71	1971-72	1972-73
Tacha, Ron*	Norton	KS	1967-68	1968-69	1969-70	1970-71
Tanner, Raymond	St. John	KS	1939-40			

K-State Wrestler	Hometown	State	Year 1	Year 2	Year 3	Year 4
Taylor, D.N.	Topeka	KS	1924-25			
Taylor, Richard	Topeka	KS	1972-73	1973-74	1974-75	
Teagarden, George	La Cygne	KS	1962-63			
Teagarden, R.R.	La Cygne	KS	1932-33			
Tempero, Benjamin	Clay Center	KS	1937-38	1938-39	1940-41	
Tempero, Floyd "Whitey"	Broughton	KS	1928-29	1929-30	1930-31	1931-32
Thacker, Robert	Hutchinson	KS	1965-66			
Thaller, Howard	Manhattan	KS	1927-28	1928-29		
Thaw, Larry	Newton	KS	1973-74	1974-75		
Thiele, Art (A.R.)	Bremen	KS	1931-32	1932-33	1933-34	
Thomas, Daniel	Ludell (Atwood)	KS	1966-67	1967-68	1968-69	
Thomas, Ivan	Garden City	KS	1933-34			
Thomas, Wilson (W.B.)	Clay Center	KS	1933-34	1935-36		
Thompson, A.C.	Mulberry	KS	1929-30			
Thompson, John*	Goodland	KS	1959-60	1960-61	1961-62	1962-63
Thurow, L	Macksville	KS	1929-30			
Tibbetts, Benton	Densmore	KS	1953-54			
Tilley, Victor	Frankfort	KS	1948-49			
Tiner, Guy	Bonner Springs	KS	1969-70			
Tinkler, John	Russell	KS	1960-61			
Topping, Ken	St. Francis	KS	1946-47			
Torkelson, J.E.	Everest	KS	1929-30			
Townsend, Delbert	Danbury (Oberlin, KS)	NE	1939-40	1941-42		
Trowbridge, Bill	Jetmore	KS	1954-55			

K-State Wrestler	Hometown	State	Year 1	Year 2	Year 3	Year 4
Turner, Jay	Quinter	KS	1935-36			
Turner, Stacy	Pretty Prairie	KS	1969-70	1970-71	1971-72	
Turner, T.J.	Hartford	KS	1925-26			
Uhrich, Randall	Beloit	KS	1966-67			
Unruh, David	Wichita (East High)	KS	1960-61	1961-62	1962-63	1963-64
Urban, Larry	Norton	KS	1964-65			
Van Vleet, Gerald	St. Francis (Danbury, NE, Oberlin, KS)	KS	1936-37	1937-38	1938-39	1939-40
Vandervilt, Lee	Solomon	KS	1924-25			
Vavroch, James	Oberlin	KS	1939-40	1940-41	1941-42	
Veatch, E.	Ozark	MO	1933-34			
Vernon, Archie	Oberlin	KS	1946-47	1947-48	1948-49	1949-50
Vernon, Thomas	Russell	KS	1967-68			
Volpe, Frank	Junction City	KS	1973-74			
Volsky, George	Pittsfield	MA	1941-42			
Wade, Dewey	Omaha (North High)	NE	1951-52			
Wagonseller, Bill	Wichita	KS	1952-53			
Walgren, Oliver E. "Shorty"	Denver	CO	1923-24	1924-25	1925-26	
Walker, Don	Kansas City	KS	1959-60			
Walker, R.D.	Junction City	KS	1926-27			
Walter, Gary	St. Francis	KS	1969-70	1970-71	1971-72	1972-73
Walters, Billy (W.T.)	Manhattan	KS	1932-33	1934-35		
Walters, Steven	Topeka (Seaman High)	KS	1969-70	1970-71		
Warner, Carl	Whiting	KS	1935-36	1936-37	1937-38	
Warner, John (J.R.)	Whiting	KS	1928-29	1929-30	1930-31	

K-State Wrestler	Hometown	State	Year 1	Year 2	Year 3	Year 4
Warner, Paul (P.F.)	Whiting	KS	1932-33			
Washburn, Roger	Manhattan	KS	1970-71	1971-72	1972-73	
Watson, Charles	Osborne	KS	1931-32			
Watson, Gary	Salina	KS	1964-65	1965-66	1966-67	
Watson, George	Clifton	KS	1933-34			
Watson, Horace	Lake City	KS	1938-39			
Way, Ben	Manhattan	KS	1948-49			
Wayman, Randal	Topeka	KS	1973-74			
Weaver, Phillip	Salina	KS	1953-54			
Weaver, Raleigh T.	Salina	KS	1953-54			
Weaver, Ted	Salina	KS	1950-51	1951-52	1952-53	1953-54
Webster, Max	Newton	KS	1950-51	1952-53		
Wegman, Edward	Hoxie	KS	1960-61	1961-62		
Weiner, Bernie	Irvington	NJ	1938-39	1939-40		
Weirick, R.T.	Olathe	KS	1929-30			
Wellman, William	St. Francis	KS	1938-39			
Wempe, Leo	Frankfort	KS	1939-40	1941-42		
Wenger, Dwight	Oberlin (Dresden)	KS	1946-47			
Wetlaufer, W.D.	Manhattan	KS	1932-33			
Wheatcroft, Kenneth	Redwing	KS	1946-47			
White, Darryl	Endwell	NY	1965-66			
White, Sig	Newton	KS	1972-73			
Whitney, Charles (Evan)	Norton	KS	1974-75			
Whitney, Wayne	St. George	KS	1928-29			

K-State Wrestler	Hometown	State	Year 1	Year 2	Year 3	Year 4
Wiebrecht, F.E.	Strong City	KS	1924-25			
Wieland, David	Oakley	KS	1966-67	1967-68	1968-69	1969-70
Wilber, Bill	St. Francis	KS	1949-50			
Wildman, H.	Liberal	KS	1931-32			
Williams, Bill	Topeka	KS	1964-65			
Williams, Orval	Colby	KS	1955-56			
Willis, Glenn (Billy)	Atchison	KS	1948-49			
Wilson, Lonnie	Salina	KS	1967-68			
Wilson, Mark	Ashland	KS	1937-38			
Wilson, R.K.	El Dorado	KS	1955-56			
Winfield, D.M.	Junction City	KS	1924-25			
Winger, Daniel	Thorp	WI	1957-58			
Winget, R.W.	Garden City	KS	1933-34			
Winkler, L.F.	Rozel	KS	1924-25			
Winter, Dave	Newton (Denver, CO, Leavenworth)	KS	1954-55			
Wirtz, Jack	Meade	KS	1955-56			
Wohlers, Bruce	Lake City	MN	1965-66			
Woofter, Dennis	Colby	KS	1961-62	1963-64	1964-65	
Woofter, Wayne	Colby / Colby CC	KS	1973-74			
Word, Larry	Wellington	KS	1957-58	1958-59	1959-60	1960-61
Wray, J.L.	Norton	KS	1936-37			
Wudtke, Ronald	Norton	KS	1962-63			
Yandell, G.O.	Wilson	KS	1924-25			
Yarnell, Clarence (Erwin)	Clarksburg	MO	1946-47			

K-State Wrestler	Hometown	State	Year 1	Year 2	Year 3	Year 4
Yoos, Kenneth "Popeye"	Atwood	KS	1936-37	1938-39		
Young, C.	Utica	KS	1931-32			
Young, Charles	Oberlin	KS	1950-51	1951-52	1953-54	
Young, Claude	Utica	KS	1933-34	1934-35		
Young, Dennis	Kansas City	KS	1965-66			
Youngers, Billy	Wichita (West High)	KS	1955-56	1956-57	1957-58	1958-59
Younger, Leon	WaKeeney / Colby CC	KS	1973-74	1974-75		
Zahner, Pat	Shawnee Mission (North High)	KS	1973-74			
Zaiss, Craig	Overland Park	KS	1966-67			
Zerbe, Lester (L.A.)	Salina	KS	1934-35	1935-36		

*Fifth year wrestlers. The following wrestlers were in the program for a fifth year

Wrestler	Fifth year
Cheynet, Jerry	1965-66
DeMoss, Richard, Jr.	1964-65
Dietrich, James	1962-63
Ellis, Ken	1957-58
Garcia, Rosalio "Gus"	1963-64
Hemmerling, Dwight	1970-71
Jackson, Wayne	1973-74
Mancuso, Bob	1955-56
McClellan, Verle (V.O.)	1947-48
Sherar, Willard J. "Pete"	1936-37
Tacha, Ron	1971-72
Thompson, John	1963-64

The 1930-31 team finished in third place at the NCAA championships. Coach Buel "Pat" Patterson (second row, far left) was in his fourth year as head coach after his outstanding career on Ed Gallagher's teams at Oklahoma A&M.
Photo Credit: Collegiate Media Group.

1971-72 team picture, Fritz Knorr's final season as head coach. Back row (l-r): Roger Fisher, Steve Fergerson, Terry Holliman, Mark Jackson, Wayne Jackson, Doug Stueve, Dale Samuelson. Middle row (l-r): Fritz Knorr, Dennis Switzky, Gary Reinhert, Barry Madden, Patrick DeBold, Ricky Flowers. Front row (l-r): Ron Tacha, Gary Walter, Bill Keller, Charles Meyer, Frank Miller, Roger Washburn, Stacy Turner
Photo Credit: Collegian Media Group.

The 1952-53 varsity team. The last team coach by Leon "Red" Reynard. He left after six years as head coach. Fritz Knorr began is nineteen-year tenure as head coach the next season. Photo (l-r): Bob Mancuso, Max Webster, Richard Spring, Ken Spicher, Bill Boon, Leslie Kramer, Leonard Pacha, Ted Weaver, Ron Marciniak.
Photo Credit: Collegian Media Group.

Father and sons; Ed, Bill, and Tom Keller. Ed's brother Elton and his son Dan were also on the team as was Ed's youngest son, Richard. The Kellers of St. Francis spanned the K-State wrestling roster from 1935-73.
Photo Credit: Tom Keller collection.

The Fansher family of Edmond, Oklahoma
Back row (l-r): Farland, Forrest, Stan, Marvin. Front row (l-r): Francis, Ray, Bernice, Virginia.

The Ray and Bernice Fansher family of Edmond, Oklahoma, bridged a connection to K-State and the wrestling program like no other family. Starting with Forrest, who was encouraged to enroll by his boss and mentor in the dairy business, all four sons attended Kansas State and wrestled for the Wildcats.

Forrest enrolled in 1933. Farland followed in 1935. In the 1940s, Marvin and Stan became Wildcats. Forrest won a Big 6 title in 1935. Farland was a 1940 NCAA qualifier. In both 1947 and 1948, Stan competed in the NCAA tournament. He was a Big 6 Champion under Coach Patterson in 1947 and a Big 7 Champion the following year under new coach Red Reynard.

The Fansher daughters were also college graduates. Virginia earned her degree from the University of Oklahoma; Frances from Oklahoma A&M. Education was important to the family. "Growing up, grandma and grandpa stressed the importance of education and reading. Even late in life, my dad was a reader and was still recommending books for me to read," said Dawn Powell (Stan's daughter).

All four boys went on to successful careers in the agricultural sector. The youngest three fought in WWII. Farland was a Naval pilot, Marvin was in the Navy, and Stan enlisted after Pearl Harbor and became part of the Army Air Corps. If not for a 3A deferment, Forrest would likely have also been part of the war effort. When the US entered the war, he was married with an infant daughter, Nancy. *Photo Credit*: Dawn Powell family collection.

To date, Kansas State University has had thirteen Rhodes Scholars. Paul Pfeutze was a member of the K-State wrestling team from 1924-26 and the first Rhodes Scholar from K-State in 1928. He was also president of the student body. He went on to a distinguished career as a professor at Vassar College. *Photo Credit*: Archives and Special Collections, Vassar College Library.

1969 grad James McDougal with Coach Knorr.
Photo Credit: Collegian Media Group.

East St. Louis native, Ellis Rainsberger, was a standout football player at K-State and was also on the Wildcat's wrestling team from 1954-57.
Photo Credit: Collegian Media Group.

In 1975, Rainsberger was named head football coach at K-State, a post he held for three years. *Photo Credit*: Collegian Media Group

Appendix C: NCAA Qualifiers and All-Americans

Qualifying for the NCAA wrestling tournament was not a requirement until 1969. Before a qualifying system, coaches simply entered individuals they felt worthy of a place in the national tournament. "National Tournament Participant" rather than the earned title of "National Qualifier" may be a more appropriate term for the early years. For this book, those that participated in the NCAA tournament are considered "National Qualifiers," even though many did not go through a qualification process. Others may have met the qualifying standard, but are not national qualifiers because they did not participate in the NCAA tournament.

Interestingly, some worthy candidates for the Wildcats did not enter the national tournament in the early years simply because they could not afford to pay their way. Awareness and budgetary considerations were not what they are today.

A rather complicated system is currently in place to determine NCAA qualifiers at the DI level. The two ways to qualify for NCAAs are through conference tournaments or an at-large selection process.

Conferences earn allotments for each weight based on regular-season performance, rankings, and Ratings Percentage Index (RPI), a combination of winning percentage, strength of schedule, and opponent's strength of schedule. The allocations for each weight class at each conference are announced late in the season before the qualifying events. The at-large selections are determined after the conference qualifiers are completed. A committee determines who is in based on the individual's body of work from the season.

Earning a place on the podium (or All-American status) at the NCAA tournament has also evolved. The progression of All-American distinction from the first NCAA-recognized tournament in 1928 through the 2024 tournament follows.

1928-40	Top-three earned All-American status
1941-62	Top-four earned All-American status
1963-78	Top-six earned All-American status
1979-present	Top-eight earned All-American status

Bracketing has also changed over the years. By far the most unusual was in 1948. "The 1948 National Collegiate Tournament will be held under Olympic Rules. This is done to coordinate our efforts with the U.S. Olympic Wrestling Committee."[1] Wrestlers, coaches, and spectators were confused by the bracketing system and how matches were scored in the tournament held on the campus of Lehigh University in Bethlehem, Pennsylvania.

The '48 tournament may be why our "folkstyle" or "collegiate style" of wrestling remained the standard rather than opting to transition to the international style of freestyle. The idea behind the change was to prepare our wrestlers to compete better on the international stage of the Olympics. However, the rule changes were not even implemented until the national tournament during the 1947-48 season. Imagine going through the entire season (and career) under the usual set of folkstyle rules, then being thrown into an entirely different set of rules for the biggest tournament of your career.

Match length was fifteen minutes; a six-minute opening period followed by three, three-minute periods compared to the three, three minute periods that athletes and coaches were accustomed to. Maybe the most dramatic change was how the fall was earned. The touch-fall replaced the 'three-second fall' that was the rule of the day in college wrestling. This caused for a few major upsets in the tournament. Traditional bracketing was replaced with the international 'black mark' system. Weight classes were even different. There were eight in both systems, but none of them were the same!

Interestingly, former K-State and then Nebraska coach Buel "Pat" Patterson was heavily involved in implementing and communicating the change. During the 1947-48 season, he was the Chairman of the NCAA wrestling rules committee, part of the United States Olympic Wrestling team's administrative staff, and editor of *The Official National Collegiate Athletic Association Wrestling Guide,* which was responsible for getting the word out and explaining the reasoning behind the change.

In the 1949 Guide, Patterson included the following in his editorial regarding the previous season's national tournament: "Unlike the usual tournaments, Olympic rules were used and both contestants and spectators were greatly confused over the technicalities." He went on to write, "It is the consensus of opinion of all concerned that a much better tournament would have been had under our American rules."[2] An interesting statistic came out of the 1948 NCAAs. A new record for the number of falls in the NCAA tournament was established at one hundred one. With only one hundred seventy total bouts, that makes for an astounding 59% of matches ending in a fall.

One of those falls happened in the 125.5-pound weight class when 1946 NCAA champion and Outstanding Wrestler award winner, Gerald "Germ" Leeman of Iowa State Teacher's College lost his only match while representing the Panthers. Detailed in *Tough Street* by James Drew, Leeman was dominating Gene McDonald from Michigan State when a touch-fall was called after Leeman rolled across his shoulders while engaged in action attempting to increase his score.[3] Due to earning his fifth black mark, he was out of the competition. Leeman went on to earn a silver medal at the 1948 Olympics in London.

The path to earning a place in the medal rounds has also changed over the years.

The early tournaments implemented a true-second where the wrestler that lost in the finals had to face the consolation champion, if they had not previously met in the tournament, to determine the runner-up.

From 1941-71, if you lost in the preliminary rounds, the opponent that beat you had to make it to the finals. From 1972-85 your victorious opponent had to earn a spot in the semifinals for you to compete in the consolation bracket.

If you were beaten in the opening round from 1986-95, your opponent had to win in the round of 16 to compete in the consolation bracket. Double elimination[4] as it exists today was not implemented until 1996.

The number of weight classes has also changed over the years. From 1928 until 1951, eight weights were contested at the NCAAs, except for 1928, 1932, and 1936, when there were seven. From 1952 to the present, ten weight classes have been contested, except for 1966 through 1969, when there were eleven.

The bracket size has also changed. The current thirty-three contestants in each bracket began in 2017, with the seeding of all thirty-three wrestlers starting in 2019.

Kansas State had one hundred twenty-one national qualifiers, with fourteen individuals earning sixteen All-American honors. Bob Mancuso is the only four-time national qualifier in K-State wrestling history. Hugh Errington (who placed third in 1930 and 1931 at heavyweight) and Ted Weaver (third place in 1952 and fourth place in 1954 at 177 pounds) are the only multiple-time All-Americans. The Pat Patterson and Fritz Knorr eras accounted for fourteen All-American honors, with the Red Reynard era accounting for the other two.

NCAA Qualifiers and All-Americans

Year	Wrestlers	Weight	Place	Coaches
1930	**Hugh Errington**	**UNL**	**3rd**	**Patterson**
1930	Joe Fickel	135	Qualf	Patterson
1931	**Bill Doyle**	**145**	**1st**	**Patterson**
1931	**Hugh Errington**	**UNL**	**3rd**	**Patterson**
1931	**Joe Fickel**	**126**	**3rd**	**Patterson**
1931	**John Richardson**	**155**	**2nd**	**Patterson**
1932	June Roberts	158	Qualf	Patterson
1935	Richard Campbell	135	Qualf	Patterson
1935	Gene Howe	145	Qualf	Patterson
1935	Dean Swift	175	Qualf	Patterson
1935	Claude Young	165	Qualf	Patterson
1937	Walter Carleton	165	Qualf	Patterson
1937	Clifford Duncan	135	Qualf	Patterson
1937	Dale Duncan	145	Qualf	Patterson
1937	John Harrison	UNL	Qualf	Patterson
1937	**Ernest Jessup**	**155**	**2nd**	**Patterson**
1937	Fred Leimbrock	118	Qualf	Patterson
1937	Carl Warner	126	Qualf	Patterson
1940	Keith Collins	165	Qualf	Patterson
1940	Glenn Duncan	145	Qualf	Patterson
1940	Farland Fansher	121	Qualf	Patterson
1940	Verle McClelland	136	Qualf	Patterson
1940	**Leon Reynard**	**175**	**3rd**	**Patterson**
1941	Glenn Duncan	145	Qualf	Patterson
1941	**Leland Porter**	**155**	**2nd**	**Patterson**
1942	**Paul Chronister**	**175**	**3rd**	**Patterson**

NCAA Qualifiers and All-Americans			
Year	Wrestlers	Weight	Place	Coaches
1942	Mel Stiefel	121	Qualf	Patterson
1942	Leo Wempe	155	Qualf	Patterson
1947	Stan Fansher	145	Qualf	Patterson
1948	Stan Fansher	147	Qualf	Reynard
1949	William Clary	175	Qualf	Reynard
1949	**Charles Lyons**	**165**	**4th**	**Reynard**
1949	Archie Vernon	136	Qualf	Reynard
1950	Joe Blanchard	UNL	Qualf	Reynard
1950	Frank Soloman	175	Qualf	Reynard
1952	Leslie Kramer	157	Qualf	Reynard
1952	Bob Mancuso	123	Qualf	Reynard
1952	**Ted Weaver**	**177**	**3rd**	**Reynard**
1953	Leslie Kramer	157	Qualf	Reynard
1953	Bob Mancuso	123	Qualf	Reynard
1954	John Cedarberg	167	Qualf	Knorr
1954	Elton Chatfield	137	Qualf	Knorr
1954	**Ken Ellis**	**UNL**	**4th**	**Knorr**
1954	Joe Landholm	115	Qualf	Knorr
1954	Bob Mancuso	130	Qualf	Knorr
1954	Ken Spicher	147	Qualf	Knorr
1954	**Ted Weaver**	**177**	**4th**	**Knorr**
1954	Charles Young	157	Qualf	Knorr
1955	Roland Alexander	147	Qualf	Knorr
1955	Ken Ellis	UNL	Qualf	Knorr
1956	Roland Alexander	147	Qualf	Knorr
1956	Dale Blume	157	Qualf	Knorr

226

NCAA Qualifiers and All-Americans

Year	Wrestlers	Weight	Place	Coaches
1956	Marvin Everest	137	Qualf	Knorr
1956	Gary Haller	177	Qualf	Knorr
1956	Bob Mancuso	130	Qualf	Knorr
1957	Jim Dietrich	191	Qualf	Knorr
1957	John (Pat) Doyle	157	Qualf	Knorr
1957	Gary Haller	177	Qualf	Knorr
1957	Jim Miller	123	Qualf	Knorr
1957	Jim Roberts	147	Qualf	Knorr
1957	Bill Youngers	115	Qualf	Knorr
1958	John (Pat) Doyle	157	Qualf	Knorr
1958	Gary Haller	177	Qualf	Knorr
1958	Jim Miller	123	Qualf	Knorr
1959	Jerry Allen	167	Qualf	Knorr
1959	**Don Darter**	**UNL**	**4th**	**Knorr**
1959	John Dooley	115	Qualf	Knorr
1959	Clair "Dee" Gard	147	Qualf	Knorr
1959	Larry Word	137	Qualf	Knorr
1960	John Dooley	115	Qualf	Knorr
1960	Clair "Dee" Gard	147	Qualf	Knorr
1960	Larry Word	137	Qualf	Knorr
1961	Rosalio "Gus" Garcia	130	Qualf	Knorr
1961	Joe Seay	147	Qualf	Knorr
1962	John Fettes	130	Qualf	Knorr
1962	Joe Seay	147	Qualf	Knorr
1962	Denton Smith	191	Qualf	Knorr
1962	Dave Unruh	123	Qualf	Knorr

NCAA Qualifiers and All-Americans

Year	Wrestlers	Weight	Place	Coaches
1963	Rosalio "Gus" Garcia	130	Qualf	Knorr
1963	Joe Seay	147	Qualf	Knorr
1963	John Thompson	137	Qualf	Knorr
1963	Dave Unruh	123	Qualf	Knorr
1964	Rosalio "Gus" Garcia	130	Qualf	Knorr
1964	John Thompson	137	Qualf	Knorr
1965	Richard DeMoss	157	Qualf	Knorr
1965	Martin Little	123	Qualf	Knorr
1966	**Bill Brown**	**152**	**6th**	**Knorr**
1966	**Jerry Cheynet**	**137**	**6th**	**Knorr**
1966	Lee Dale	145	Qualf	Knorr
1966	Larry Elder	160	Qualf	Knorr
1966	Russell Lay	130	Qualf	Knorr
1966	Martin Little	123	Qualf	Knorr
1967	Bill Brown	152	Qualf	Knorr
1967	Russell Lay	123	Qualf	Knorr
1967	James McDougal	130	Qualf	Knorr
1967	Dan Thomas	145	Qualf	Knorr
1968	Gary Richards	160	Qualf	Knorr
1969	Marv Landes	123	Qualf	Knorr
1969	Alan Maestas	130	Qualf	Knorr
1969	James McDougal	137	Qualf	Knorr
1969	Gary Richards	160	Qualf	Knorr
1969	Ron Tacha	177	Qualf	Knorr
1969	Dave Wieland	167	Qualf	Knorr
1970	Jim Barrett	134	Qualf	Knorr

NCAA Qualifiers and All-Americans

Year	Wrestlers	Weight	Place	Coaches
1970	Lyle Cook	142	Qualf	Knorr
1970	Alan Maestas	126	Qualf	Knorr
1970	Ron Tacha	190	Qualf	Knorr
1970	Dave Wieland	158	Qualf	Knorr
1971	Steve Fergerson	118	Qualf	Knorr
1971	Dwight Hemmerling	UNL	Qualf	Knorr
1971	Ron Tacha	190	Qualf	Knorr
1972	Wayne Jackson	134	Qualf	Knorr
1972	Dale Samuelson	142	Qualf	Knorr
1973	Wayne Jackson	134	Qualf	Samuelson
1974	Phil Donley	177	Qualf	Fozzard
1974	Wayne Jackson	134	Qualf	Fozzard
1974	John Kadel	167	Qualf	Fozzard
1974	Wayne Woofter	UNL	Qualf	Fozzard
1975	Bruce Randall	142	Qualf	Fozzard

Jerry Cheynet (right) is congratulated by Coach Fritz Knorr on his 1966 All-American finish. Fellow 1966 All American, Bill Brown, looks on. *Photo Credit*: Collegian Media Group.

Bob Mancuso, 1956 grad, is the only four-time national qualifier in K-State wrestling history. *Photo Credit*: Collegian Media Group.

Dale, Clifford, and Glen Duncan (standing, top, bottom) of St. Francis were all NCAA qualifiers for Kansas State. Dale and Clifford qualified in 1937, Glen in 1940 and 1941. *Photo Credit*: The Norman Transcript.

Ted Weaver is one of only two, two-time All-Americans in K-State wrestling history. He finished in third place in 1952 and in fourth place in 1954 at 177 pounds at the NCAA tournament. *Photo Credit*: Collegian Media Group.

Hugh Errington finished in third place at heavyweight at both the 1930 and 1931 NCAA tournaments. He is the first All-American in K-State wrestling history. *Photo Credit*: Collegian Media Group.

Ron Tacha (top) qualified for the NCAAs in 1969 (177 pounds), 1970, and 1971 (190 pounds). He is one of only five K-State wrestlers that participated in three NCAA tournaments. *Photo Credit*: Collegian Media Group.

Leon "Red" Reynard (wearing suit) earned All-American honors for the Cats when he placed third at the 1940 NCAA championships at 175 pounds. In 1947 he began a six-year stint as K-State's head coach when his coach, Pat Patterson, left for the University of Nebraska. In the photo, Gerald Hackney is on top of Bill Clary as Coach Reynard instructs. *Photo Credit*: Collegian Media Group.

Appendix C Endnotes: *NCAA Qualifiers and All-Americans*

1. *The Official National Collegiate Athletic Association Wrestling Guide 1948*, p. 32.
2. 1949 The Official National Collegiate Athletic Association Wrestling Guide, p. 14
3. *Tough Streets: From Osage to London to Lehigh, the Remarkable Life of Gerald "Germ" Leeman* by James Drew, p. 77-83. In a bizarre repercussion of the international bracketing rules used at the 1948 NCAAs, Rometo "Rummy" Macias of Iowa, who was a fellow competitor in the 125.5 pound weight class, won his finals match, yet finished as runner-up. Macias, Leeman, Paul McDaniel of Oklahoma State, and champion George Lewis of Waynesburg all had a loss in the tournament. Leeman didn't place, but Michigan State's McDonald went 3-2 and placed fourth. The well-intentioned system was confusing, frustrating, and unjust then and even nearly eight decades removed.
4. Double elimination is also referred to as full-wrestlebacks.

Appendix D: Kids State

The USA Wrestling-Kansas (USAWKS) Kids Folkstyle State Tournament is one of the largest multi-day sporting events in Kansas each year. The event has been a fixture on the state's wrestling calendar for many years, drawing an increasing number of competitors and enthusiasts.

The tournament began in 1964 at Manhattan High School with 127 competitors from nineteen Kansas communities who came together for a two-day tournament held on two mats on March 5-6. Since then, the event has grown significantly, with a record 2,446 competitors from 187 clubs from across the state participating in the tournament held on eighteen mats in Topeka, March 8-10, 2024.

Fritz Knorr enrolled at Kansas State University in the fall of 1927, the same year that Buel "Pat" Patterson began coaching at K-State. Knorr shared his mentor's philosophy of growing the sport at the grassroots level. Later, when Knorr took over as head coach, he continued to provide opportunities for coaches to learn, athletes to compete, and fans to watch. In 1956, he revived and expanded the coach's clinic that Patterson had started in 1939. The clinic has included Knorr's name since his death in 1972. The KWCA Fritz Knorr Fall Clinic is nearing its seventieth consecutive year of providing a pre-season clinic for Kansas high school coaches.

About a decade after the annual coaching clinic was established, Knorr hosted the first kids' state tournament. After the initial year at Manhattan High, the event was moved to the K-State campus, where it was held in Nichols Hall from 1965-68 and Ahearn Fieldhouse from 1969-74.

The 1973 tournament, however, was held at Henry Levitt Arena on the campus of Wichita State University. Due to Coach Knorr's death, graduate assistant Dale Samuelson covering for the 1972-73 season, and the Fred Fozzard hire in April 1973, it was too much for K-State to take on during that time.

Since the tournament's early years, Knorr served as the tournament manager; overseeing details from registration to weigh-ins and bracketing to set-up and clean-up. The members of the K-State team were also vested in pulling off the event each year, providing the muscle to set up and roll up the mats, and helping work tables and officiate.

The tournament bounced around to different communities over the years, such as Wichita, Salina, and Hays, until it settled in Topeka in 1992 at the Kansas Expocentre. The event has taken place in Topeka every year since then, except for 2020 when it was canceled due to COVID-19[1] and again in 2021, when the tournament was moved to the Kansas Star Arena in Mulvane due to continued COVID restrictions in Topeka. From 2022-24, the Capital City hosted the event again, this time at the newly renovated and renamed Stormont Vail Events Center. In 2022, the tournament also introduced an all-girls division.

The event that started on two mats in a high school gym in 1964 has grown into a 7,500-seat arena with eighteen mats and participant numbers that exceed many of the towns those competitors hail from.

The Kansas Kids' State tournament was established in 1964. The first tournament was a two-day event held at Manhattan High School on two mats. The three-day tournament in 2024 used eighteen mats and hosted a record 2,446 entries.
Photo Credit: Keith Horinek.

Former USAWKS State Chairperson, Will Cokeley, has been involved in the sport since his youth in Liberal and has been heavily involved in USAWKS leadership for many years. "Kansas State University is strongly tied to the development of youth wrestling in the state. I'm convinced that USAWKS is in a strong financial position with robust membership numbers due to the foundation put in place so many years ago under the leadership of coaches like Buel Patterson and Fritz Knorr," he said.

Kansas Kids' State 1964-2025			
Year	City	Location	Date
2025*	Topeka	Stormont Vail Events Center	March 14-16, 2025
2024	Topeka	Stormont Vail Events Center	March 8-10, 2024
2023	Topeka	Stormont Vail Events Center	March 10-12, 2023
2022	Topeka	Stormont Vail Events Center	March 11-13, 2022
2021	Mulvane	Kansas Star Arena	March 12-14, 2021
2020	Topeka (Cancelled due to COVID)	Kansas Expocentre	March 14-15, 2020 (scheduled for)
2019	Topeka	Kansas Expocentre	March 16-17, 2019
2018	Topeka	Kansas Expocentre	March 24-25, 2018
2017	Topeka	Kansas Expocentre	March 25-26, 2017
2016	Topeka	Kansas Expocentre	March 25-26, 2016
2015	Topeka	Kansas Expocentre	March 28-29, 2015
2014	Topeka	Kansas Expocentre	March 29-30, 2014
2013	Topeka	Kansas Expocentre	March 29-30, 2013
2012	Topeka	Kansas Expocentre	March 24-25, 2012
2011	Topeka	Kansas Expocentre	March 26-27, 2011
2010	Topeka	Kansas Expocentre	March 27-28, 2010
2009	Topeka	Kansas Expocentre	March 28-29, 2009
2008	Topeka	Kansas Expocentre	March 29-30, 2008
2007	Topeka	Kansas Expocentre	March 24-25, 2007
2006	Topeka	Kansas Expocentre	March 25-26, 2006
2005	Topeka	Kansas Expocentre	March 25-26, 2005
2004	Topeka	Kansas Expocentre	March 27-28, 2004

Kansas Kids' State 1964-2025			
Year	City	Location	Date
2003	Topeka	Kansas Expocentre	March 29-30, 2003
2002	Topeka	Kansas Expocentre	March 29-30, 2002
2001	Topeka	Kansas Expocentre	March 24-25, 2001
2000	Topeka	Kansas Expocentre	March 25-26, 2000
1999	Topeka	Kansas Expocentre	March 27-28, 1999
1998	Topeka	Kansas Expocentre	March 28-29, 1998
1997	Topeka	Kansas Expocentre	March 28-29, 1997
1996	Topeka	Kansas Expocentre	March 30-31, 1996
1995	Topeka	Kansas Expocentre	March 23-24, 1995
1994	Topeka	Kansas Expocentre	March 26-27, 1994
1993	Topeka	Kansas Expocentre	March 27-28, 1993
1992	Topeka	Kansas Expocentre	March 28-29, 1992
1991	Salina	Bicentennial Center	March 29-30, 1991
1990	Salina	Bicentennial Center	March 24-25, 1990
1989	Salina	Bicentennial Center	March 24-25, 1989
1988	Salina	Bicentennial Center	March 26-27, 1988
1987	Salina	Bicentennial Center	March 28-29, 1987
1986	Salina	Bicentennial Center	March 28-29, 1986
1985	Topeka	Washburn University	March 30-31, 1985
1984	Salina	Bicentennial Center	April 20-21, 1984
1983	Ft. Hays	Gross Memorial	April 1-2, 1983
1982	Salina	Bicentennial Center	April 9-10, 1982
1981	Salina	Bicentennial Center	April 17-18, 1981
1980	Ft. Hays	Gross Memorial	April 11-12, 1980
1979	Ft. Hays	Gross Memorial	April 13-14, 1979
1978	Ft. Hays	Gross Memorial	April 21-22, 1978

Kansas Kids' State 1964-2025			
Year	City	Location	Date
1977	Wichita	Henry Levitt Arena	April 15-16, 1977
1976	Wichita	Henry Levitt Arena	April 16-17, 1976
1975	Wichita	Henry Levitt Arena	April 18-19, 1995
1974	Manhattan	Ahearn Fieldhouse	April 19-20, 1974
1973	Wichita	Henry Levitt Arena	*Unconfirmed*
1972	Manhattan	Ahearn Fieldhouse	April 14-15, 1972
1971	Manhattan	Ahearn Fieldhouse	April 16-17, 1971
1970	Manhattan	Ahearn Fieldhouse	April 10-11, 1970
1969	Manhattan	Ahearn Fieldhouse	April 11-12, 1969
1968	Manhattan	Nichols Hall	March 15-16, 1968
1967	Manhattan	Nichols Hall	March 24-25, 1967
1966	Manhattan	Nichols Hall	March 18-19, 1966
1965	Manhattan	Nichols Hall	March 20, 1965
1964	Manhattan	Manhattan High School	March 5-6, 1964

*The contract for the next bid cycle has been approved. The tournament will remain in Topeka through 2030.

Appendix D Endnotes: *Kids State*

1. With mats laid out and score clocks wired for action, the tournament was canceled by county and city officials on Thursday, March 12, 2020, the day before the three-day extravaganza was to begin. A press conference that was aired live explained that the risks were too great given information from the Kansas Health Department.

Appendix E: Northwest Kansas League

The influence of professional wrestling on the sport's popularity in Kansas can't be ignored when considering the forces that brought about the advent of sanctioned high school wrestling in Kansas.

As mentioned in the opening chapter, the sport was a popular attraction throughout the state at the turn of the century and nowhere more so than in Wichita.

Professional matches were commonplace and a regular source of local entertainment in the late 1800s through the early part of the next century. In the spring of 1922, Fairmount College (later Wichita State) added wrestling to its athletic department when the popular pro, Dick Daviscourt, permanently moved to Wichita and was named coach at Fairmount College to introduce the sport to its students. Area high school students were also invited to learn under the pro's tutelage.

On March 3, 1922, Wichita was the focal point of the sport when the world heavyweight wrestling championship bout was held at the Forum in the downtown area.

A capacity crowd of 6,000 saw Ed "Strangler" Lewis defeat Stanislaus Zbyszko for the title. Zbyszko had previously twice defeated Lewis at matches held at Madison Square Garden. Jack Dempsey, the popular heavyweight boxing champion, drew only 2,000 spectators when he fought in Wichita in 1922. To be fair, Dempsey's bouts were little more than glorified practice sessions, but the wrestling crowd demonstrates Wichita's status in the wrestling world and the ability to attract a large gate.

Wichita High School was renamed Wichita High School East in 1929 when Wichita North opened its doors. The Blue Aces, as East came to be known after the split, had an organized wrestling team as early as the 1921-22 school year. The early adoption was influenced by Daviscourt's presence at Fairmount College and the awareness of school officials that wrestling was gaining popularity at the scholastic level on the East Coast.

One of Wichita High's faculty advocates had a strong connection to the top college program in the land. Clifford Gallagher, brother of

Oklahoma A&M's head coach, Ed, was hired by the school in 1922 as PE teacher and track coach. By 1926 he was named athletic director. In 1925, Clifford made arrangements for A&M to travel to WHS for an exhibition to help promote the sport.[1]

The Ark Valley League hosted the state's first league wrestling tournament on February 13, 1926, when teams from Arkansas City, El Dorado, Hutchinson, Newton, Wichita, Wellington, and Winfield gathered in the gym at Wichita High.

Wichita won the inaugural tournament by crowning champions in six out of the seven weight classes. El Dorado was runner-up, followed by Hutchinson, Winfield, and Newton. Neither Arkansas City nor Wellington scored a team point. Kingman, also in the league, did not participate. It was reported that "Coach Herzer was busy coaching the basketball team and did not have time to coach any boys in wrestling."[2]

There were other pockets of wrestling activity in Kansas at the time, but Wichita and the Ark Valley were the clear early adopters of wrestling as a formal sporting activity at the high school level in Kansas. However, the rural schools of the northwest part of the state were not far behind.

Coach Buel "Pat" Patterson and Kansas State University oversaw the establishment, growth, and development of wrestling programs at the high school level in an area of the state that valued the traits of hard work and physical activity which meshed with the sport of wrestling.

From hosting invitationals and the early years of the state tournament to stirring up interest at the grassroots level, Pat had a vision and a plan to bring the sport to the level he was accustomed to when growing up in Oklahoma and going through Ed Gallagher's program at Oklahoma A&M.

The story of wrestling In Kansas, especially at Kansas State University, can only be told by mentioning the influence of the Northwest Kansas League (NWKL).

Throughout K-State's wrestling history, the NWKL was a recruiting stronghold for the Wildcats. Many of those recruits had successful college careers and then went on to coach at the high school level, several back in the NWKL.

A study of the roster list in Appendix B shows that approximately 17 percent of the individuals who populated the cumulative roster hailed from a high school in the NWKL.[3] Of the eighty-six unique NCAA qualifiers and All-Americans to K-State's credit, almost a third came from NWKL schools. Even considering the Wichita and Kansas City population centers and hometown Manhattan, St. Francis, Norton, Oberlin, and Goodland out of the NWKL all rank in the top ten for hometowns represented on the historic K-State wrestling roster.

The Northwest Kansas League, established in 1927, was made up of schools in counties that border Nebraska to the north and Colorado to the west, defining the northwest corner of the Sunflower State. Those counties, Cheyenne, Decatur, Logan, Norton, Rawlins, Sheridan, Sherman, and Thomas, housed the seven charter members of the NWKL: Atwood, Colby, Goodland, Hoxie, Norton,[4] Decatur Community (Oberlin), and St. Francis. Oakley joined in 1951.

With a series of home and away duals starting in 1924, before the NWKL was even established, Norton and Oberlin led the way in adapting the sport. Oberlin hosted and won the first league wrestling tournament on February 23, 1930. Norton, Goodland, Hoxie, and Atwood followed in the team standings.

By 1975, K-State's final season, all eight schools had at least one state title to their credit. As of 2024, that group has accumulated an incredible *seventy-one* state championships.

There have been some eye-popping results at the state tournament for the NWKL, but none as impressive as what happened in the 1970s. In the five state tournaments from 1971-74 and 1976, league schools captured titles in *both* 2-1A and 3A. In three of the five years, both runners-up also came from the NWKL.

The results of the 1971 state tournament are hard to believe. That year, all eight schools finished in the top six of their class. In 3A, Oberlin won the title, Norton was runner-up, Colby finished in fourth place, and Goodland was fifth. In 2-1A it was a trophy sweep, with Hoxie winning the title, Oakley taking runner-up honors, and Atwood finishing third. St. Francis finished in sixth place.

Coach Buzz Matson and his Decatur Community High School wrestlers ran the table during the 1970-71 season at a time when dual results determined league standings. The Red Devils finished 7-0 in the NWKL and 8-0 overall.

Jake Durham's Norton Bluejays, defending NWKL and state champion, provided the biggest challenge for Oberlin. In the early weeks of the season, the Devils came back from a 20-8 deficit to pull out the 24-20 victory. It was Oberlin's first dual win over Norton since 1962.

Individual stars that populated the K-State rosters from NWKL schools were plenty. Hugh Errington of Goodland is one of only a pair of two-time All-Americans in program history. The Duncan trio of St. Francis is part of the lore. Clifton, Dale, and Glenn all participated in the NCAA tournament. Dale went on to coach Oberlin to state titles in 1942 and 1943.[5]

Ron Tacha of Norton was a rare three-time NCAA qualifier. Bill Brown of Oberlin earned one of only sixteen All-American honors for the Cats. Elmer Hackney,[6] also out of Oberlin, left high school with two state wrestling titles and a runner-up finish. He didn't earn the wrestling accolades at K-State to match what he did in track and field and football, but he has a case for the title of "greatest athlete" in K-State history.

The first four-time state champion in Kansas history is Doug Duell of Goodland. His father, Ben, was a state medalist for the Cowboys and went on to compete for K-State from 1948-51.

Dee Gard, also of Goodland, was a star on the mat for K-State and went on to coach two state champion teams at Wichita Heights. Gus Garcia, a three-time NCAA qualifier, graduated from Douglass High School but led Atwood to a state title as its head coach and went on to a Hall of Fame career in the high school coaching ranks. Oakley native Dale Samuelson returned to his hometown after a one-year stint as interim head coach at K-State. He brought home the Plainsmen's only state wrestling championship in 1974, his first year at the helm.

As of the publication of this book, Norton leads the charter members of the NWKL with seventeen state titles, the last coming in 2020. J.R. "Jake" Durham led the program to titles in 1959, 1962, 1965, 1968, 1970, and 1973. Billy Johnson brought the Jays back to the top with titles in 2004, 2005, 2006, 2010, 2011, 2013, 2014, 2015, 2016, 2017, and 2020.

The smallest school in the NWKL, St. Francis, is next with sixteen state titles. The St. Francis dynasty is unique in that six different coaches have served as head coaches when the Indians finished as state champs. Riley Whearty was first with a title in 1938. Gilford Alexander added one in 1940. Warren "Barney" Boring's K-State career was interrupted during WWII before bringing titles to Sainty in 1949, 1952, and 1953. Under Maynard Skinner's watch, another three were added in the consecutive years of 1954, 1955, and 1956. It took another decade, but Gary "Pudge" Wilson led the school to titles in 1966 and 1967 before becoming head coach at Colby Community College. Larry Gabel piled on another six in 1978, 1979, 1980, 1984, 1996, and 1997.

Hoxie has won the most recent four 321A state titles, bringing its total to fourteen. Bill Pickinpaugh started the flood of titles at Hoxie with championships in 1969, 1971, and 1972. After an eighteen-year drought, Kirk Baker racked up seven titles in a short period: 1990, 1991, 1994, 1998, 1999, 2002, and 2003. After another eighteen-year drought, Mike Porsch returned the program to relevance with consecutive titles in 2021, 2022, 2023, and 2024.

In April 2024, after seventeen years as the program's head coach and an association that dates back to 1984 when he enrolled at Hoxie High as a freshman, Porsch announced his retirement. Assistant Ryan Etherton is set to take over as head coach. With six returning state medalists, look for Hoxie to remain in the 321A driver's seat for the foreseeable future.

Oberlin has ten titles to its credit. Bill Huey got the ball rolling in 1937. Jack Cronk added a single title in 1939. Dale Duncan led the Red Devils to back-to-back titles in 1942 and 1943. Melvin Simpson won a pair in 1957 and 1961. Gordon "Buzz" Matson was at the helm for four titles: 1971, 1975, 1976, and 1977.

Colby has six titles, with K-State alum Richard Fowler at the helm for the first in 1936. Leo Thomsen was the skipper for the 1951 championship. K-State grad Kyle Mines led the program to the 1958 title. After four decades, Mitch Beims showed the Eagles the way with a title in 2001. Head Coach Matt Sims was in charge when Colby brought home 4A titles in 2009 and 2016.

Goodland has five titles. Rocky Welton led the program for its first three titles in 1972, 1974, and 1976 before moving on to Garden City, where he led the Buffalos to six titles in the 1990s. Eddie Clark was the head coach for the 1997 title. Current Fort Hays Tech – Northwest head coach and Louisiana native Chris Guillot brought the Cowboys their latest title in 2000.

Gus Garcia's career began at Atwood after a stellar career at K-State. His Buffalos captured the 1973 state title before he moved on to Augusta. Steve Woody led the program to the 1989 title in Class 321A.

Oakley's lone title came in 1974 under Samuelson's direction.

From the mid-1970s until today, the league has undergone restructuring and does not reflect what it once was. As of this writing, the only schools still in the league that were there in 1975 are Atwood-Rawlins County, Oberlin-Decatur Community, and St. Francis.

Recent history aside, it is hard to argue that the Northwest Kansas League is a cornerstone of wrestling in Kansas. The formal development of the sport can be traced back to that sparsely populated corner of the state where accomplished athletes became coaches and moved to areas of the state where wrestling was less known. "If you wrestled in the Northwest Kansas League, you wrestled the toughest competition in the state. We knew that and felt that. There was just no doubt about it. At that time, we were the toughest league around. It made us better. People say that you need to get out and face better competition but wrestling that caliber of teams each week made everyone better. It was pretty neat competing and later coaching in that environment," said Kirk Baker.

In addition to his coaching success at Hoxie, Baker is also one of the most accomplished wrestlers in Kansas high school history. From 1973-76, he was a six-time state finalist for Goodland. He won two

3A state championships and was twice runner-up. In 1975, he was grand state runner-up and the next year, the final year of Grand State, Baker captured the 132-pound title.

1938 K-State grad Dale Duncan became the first state champion in the history of the storied St. Francis program when he won the 135-pound title in 1934. Pictured with four-time state Champion Billy Gabel in 1996 after his fourth state title.
Photo Credit: St. Francis High School (photo by Larry Gabel).

Wayne Woofter, Colby High School grad and 1974 NCAA qualifier for K-State. *Photo Credit:* Collegian Media Group Description.

Jerry Cheynet spent two years as Oakley High School's head coach before starting a college coaching career at Lake Superior State University and Virginia Tech. He coached various sports at the college level, including a season as head women's soccer coach at Tech. *Photo Credit*: Virginia Tech Athletics.

As was typical for the era, this picture of the 1940-41 lettermen is made up of about half hailing from NWKL schools: Hancock and Duncan (St. Francis), the Porter brothers (Norton), and Vavroch (Oberlin).
Photo Credit: Collegian Media Group.

Appendix E Endnotes: *Northeast Kansas League*

1. *The Wichita Eagle* (Wichita, Kansas), Saturday, January 31, 1925, page 9.
2. *Oracle* (Kingman, Kansas), Tuesday, February 23, 1926, page 1.
3. Approximately 12% of the cumulative roster came from schools associated with the Ark Valley League. The Ark Valley and NWKL combined (fifteen schools) account for nearly one-third of the names on K-State's cumulative roster. The combined leagues account for nearly 50% of K-State's National Qualifiers and All-Americans.
4. Norton left the NWKL league in 1976 to join the Mid-Continent League.
5. For more on Coach Duncan and the other K-State wrestling alums that went on to win state titles while coaching the NWKL, see Chapter 4: "LegaSeay." The other coaches are Warren Boring (St. Francis), Richard Fowler (Colby), Gus Garcia (Atwood), Kyle Mines (Colby), and Dale Samuelson (Oakley).
6. Read more about Hackney in Chapter 5: "One Man Gang," which is devoted to his incredible story.

ABOUT THE AUTHOR

Patrick Kelly spent his formative years in Britt, Iowa. He attended the University of Iowa, where he wrestled under Dan Gable, before transferring to the University of Nebraska at Omaha, finishing his college career under the guidance of Mike Denney. Kelly has written articles for several publications, including *WIN*, and has produced hundreds of podcast episodes for USA Wrestling-Kansas (USAWKS) and the Kansas Wrestling Coaches Association (KWCA). He has been a teacher and coach for thirty years and is a National Board Certified Teacher. He lives in Topeka, Kansas, with his wife Lisa. They have three grown children.

You can reach the author at: patrick.kelly.ks@gmail.com